Empowering Leadership:

A Christian Approach to Emotional

Intelligence

About the Author

In the rapidly evolving landscape of business and leadership, the author emerges as a pivotal voice, skillfully navigating the intricacies of guiding contemporary leaders towards excellence. Hailing from the vibrant shores of Virginia Beach, Virginia, the author brings to the table a rich tapestry of experience, both as a seasoned Professional Development Trainer and as a visionary entrepreneur at the helm of On Track Coaching, LLC. This unique blend of roles not only enriches her perspective but also grounds her insights in the practical realities of building and leading successful teams.

The author's expertise is not confined to a single aspect of leadership; rather, it spans a comprehensive range of subjects that are crucial for today's leaders. From the nuanced dynamics of team building and emotional intelligence to the strategic imperatives of business acumen and project management, her breadth of knowledge is both vast and deep.

Central to the author's philosophy is the belief in the transformative power of leadership that is informed by emotional intelligence and underpinned by strong business acumen. She argues persuasively that the most effective leaders are those who understand the emotional landscape of their teams and can navigate through it with empathy and strategic foresight. This approach does not merely seek to enhance the operational efficiency of organizations but aims to foster a culture of innovation, mutual respect, and sustained growth.

As a speaker on leadership, emotional intelligence, and team building, the author has garnered acclaim for her ability to engage and inspire audiences. Her talks are not just presentations but interactive experiences that challenge conventional thinking and encourage a deeper exploration of what it means to lead in the 21st century. It is this blend of critical thinking, strategic insight, and the ability to connect with people on a personal level that sets her apart as a speaker and as an author.

In her book, the author leverages her extensive experience in training leaders and her personal journey in building On Track Coaching, LLC to offer readers a comprehensive guide on navigating the challenges of modern leadership. Through a series of meticulously researched case studies, practical strategies, and reflective exercises, the book serves as a beacon for those aspiring to elevate their leadership skills. It is not just a book but a toolkit for building resilient, forward-thinking leaders who are equipped to thrive in an increasingly complex and interconnected world.

In essence, the author embodies the qualities of the leaders she seeks to cultivate: visionary, empathetic, strategically astute, and always driven by a commitment to help others succeed. Their book is not just a testament to her expertise but a reflection of her passion for unlocking the potential in every leader to create a positive and lasting impact in the world of business and beyond.

Dedication

To the diligent seeker of wisdom, who understands that true leadership is cultivated in the fertile ground of humility and service. This book is dedicated to those who aspire to lead with a heart attuned to the whispers of grace, courage molded by faith, and actions inspired by an unwavering commitment to emotional intelligence through a Christian lens. May you discover within these pages not only the principles of empowering leadership but also the transformative power of living out these truths in every facet of your life.

Let this journey illuminate the path to a leadership style that is both nurturing and powerful, grounded in the teachings of Christ, who exemplified the ultimate model of leadership through love, empathy, and self-sacrifice. May you be emboldened to lead with compassion, to listen with intention, and to serve with a heart that reflects the love of God.

In the pursuit of leadership excellence, may you find that the truest form of power lies in the ability to understand and connect with others on a deep, emotional level, and in doing so, cultivate environments where everyone is encouraged to grow and thrive. This book is a testament to the belief that leadership, at its core, is a calling to serve others through the lens of Christ's love and wisdom.

For every leader who believes in the transformative power of emotional intelligence, for every follower of Christ who seeks to lead with authenticity and grace, and for everyone in between who aspires to make a difference in their corner of the world—this book is for you. May your journey be richly blessed, and may your leadership be a beacon of hope and a source of strength to all those you are called to serve.

Acknowledgements

Crafting this exploration into the confluence of Christian principles and emotional intelligence within the sphere of leadership has been a journey of profound introspection, learning, and faith. This book is the fruit of countless hours of dedication, not only from myself but from a constellation of individuals whose support, wisdom, and encouragement have been indispensable.

First, I extend my deepest gratitude to the Divine, whose guidance and wisdom illuminate every step of our paths. The teachings of Christ serve as the bedrock upon which this work is founded, offering an inexhaustible wellspring of inspiration for leadership that is both compassionate and effective.

To my family, whose unwavering support and love provide me with the strength and motivation to pursue my passions and goals. Your belief in me and my work has been a source of comfort and encouragement throughout this endeavor. Your sacrifices have not gone unnoticed, and I am eternally grateful for your presence in my life.

I owe a debt of gratitude to my mentors and colleagues in the fields of leadership development, emotional intelligence, and theology. Your insights and critiques have been invaluable, pushing me to delve deeper and refine my thoughts and arguments. Special thanks to Dr. Zeke Brown, whose mentorship has been a guiding light in my professional journey, offering not just academic guidance but also spiritual wisdom.

To the participants of my workshops and seminars, whose questions, experiences, and reflections have enriched this work in countless ways. Your willingness to engage deeply with the material and share your journeys has added layers of depth and authenticity to this exploration.

Finally, to the reader, who embarks on this journey with an open heart and mind. This book is ultimately for you, crafted with the hope that it will offer guidance, inspiration, and a deeper understanding of what it means to lead with emotional intelligence grounded in Christian values. May you find within its pages a source of inspiration and a call to action, to lead in a way that is both transformative and deeply rooted in the teachings of Christ.

This book is a testament to the collective wisdom, support, and encouragement of each individual mentioned, and many more who have contributed in ways both big and small. To all of you, I offer my heartfelt thanks and the hope that we may continue to inspire and uplift each other in our shared journey towards empathetic and effective leadership.

Contents

Introduction:

In today's dynamic and ever-changing world, effective leadership is not merely about directing tasks or making decisions; it is about inspiring, empowering, and uplifting others to reach their fullest potential. Empowering leadership, rooted in humility, compassion, and integrity, is key to unlocking the full potential of individuals, teams, and organizations. At the heart of empowering leadership lies emotional intelligence (EI), the ability to recognize, understand, and manage our emotions and those of others.

In this book, "Empowering Leadership: A Christian Approach to Emotional Intelligence," we embark on a journey of exploration and discovery, delving into the transformative power of EI through the lens of Christian values and principles. Drawing inspiration from the timeless wisdom of Scripture and the teachings of Jesus Christ, we uncover the profound connection between emotional intelligence and effective, empowering leadership.

Through real-life examples, practical insights, and actionable strategies, this book aims to equip leaders with the knowledge and tools needed to cultivate their emotional intelligence and lead with authenticity, empathy, and purpose. Whether you are a seasoned executive, a budding entrepreneur, or a leader in any capacity, the principles outlined in these pages will empower you to elevate your leadership to new heights and make a lasting impact in the lives of those you serve.

As you embark on this journey, I invite you to embrace the challenge of exploring and applying emotional intelligence principles in your leadership role. Together, let us journey towards becoming leaders who not only excel in the boardroom but also inspire, uplift, and empower those around us, reflecting the love, grace, and wisdom of our Savior, Jesus Christ.

Chapter One:
Understanding Emotional
Intelligence

Emotional Intelligence And Its Components

Emotional intelligence (EI) is the ability to recognize, understand, manage, and effectively navigate both one's own emotions and the emotions of others. It involves a set of skills that enable individuals to develop strong interpersonal relationships, make sound decisions, and cope with the challenges of daily life. The components of emotional intelligence include:

Self-Awareness: This component involves recognizing and understanding one's own emotions, as well as their impact on thoughts, behavior, and decision-making. Self-aware individuals can accurately assess their strengths, weaknesses, values, and goals, which helps them better understand themselves and their interactions with others.

1. Psalm 139:23-24 - "Search me, O God, and know my heart: try me, and know my thoughts: And see if there be any wicked way in me, and lead me in the way everlasting." This passage reflects a prayer for God to examine the heart and thoughts of the psalmist, demonstrating a desire for self-awareness and alignment with God's will.
2. Lamentations 3:40 - "Let us search and try our ways, and turn again to the Lord." Here, the author encourages self-examination and reflection on one's actions in relation to God, suggesting a need for self-awareness and repentance.

3. 1 Corinthians 11:28 - "But let a man examine himself, and so let him eat of that bread, and drink of that cup." This verse is part of the instructions regarding observing the Lord's Supper. It highlights the importance of self-examination before participating in this sacred ritual, indicating the need for self-awareness and reflection on one's relationship with Christ.

4. 2 Corinthians 13:5 - "Examine yourselves, whether ye be in the faith; prove your own selves. Know ye, not your own selves, how that Jesus Christ is in you, except ye be reprobates?" Paul urges the Corinthians to examine themselves to ensure they live according to their faith and recognize the presence of Christ within them. This verse underscores the importance of self-awareness in spiritual matters.

5. James 1:23-25 - "For if any be a hearer of the word and not a doer, he is like unto a man beholding his natural face in a glass: For he beholdeth himself, and goeth his way, and straightway forgetteth what manner of man he was. But whoso looketh into the perfect law of liberty, and continueth therein, he being not a forgetful hearer, but a doer of the work, this man shall be blessed in his deed." This passage uses the analogy of a mirror to illustrate the importance of self-awareness in relation to the Word of God, emphasizing the need for introspection and the application of biblical principles in one's life.

While these passages may not explicitly use the term "self-awareness," they offer insights into the importance of introspection, self-examination, and understanding one's thoughts, actions, and relationship with God.

Self-Regulation: Self-regulation involves managing and controlling one's emotions, impulses, and behaviors in various situations. It involves staying calm under pressure, controlling disruptive impulses, and adapting to changing circumstances with composure. Self-regulated individuals can think before acting, handle stress effectively, and maintain a positive outlook even in challenging situations.

1. Proverbs 25:28 - "He that hath no rule over his own spirit is like a city that is broken down and without walls." This verse emphasizes the importance of self-control and managing one's emotions and impulses.

2. 1 Corinthians 9:25-27 - "And every man that strives for the mastery is temperate in all things. Now, they do it to obtain a corruptible crown, but we an incorruptible. I therefore so run, not as uncertainly; so fight I, not as one that beateth the air: But I keep under my body, and bring it into subjection: lest that by any means, when I have preached to others, I myself should be a castaway." Here, Paul uses the analogy of an athlete in training to emphasize the need for self-discipline and self-control in the Christian life.

3. Galatians 5:22-23 - "But the fruit of the Spirit is love, joy, peace, longsuffering, gentleness, goodness, faith, Meekness, temperance: against such there is no law." This passage speaks of the fruits of the Spirit, which include self-control (temperance). It implies that through the Holy Spirit, believers can develop self-management skills.

4. 2 Timothy 1:7 - "For God hath not given us the spirit of fear; but of power, and of love, and of a sound mind." While not explicitly about self-management, this verse speaks to the idea that God allows believers to exercise self-control and sound judgment.

Empathy: Empathy is the capacity to understand and share the feelings, perspectives, and experiences of others. It involves putting oneself in another person's shoes, listening attentively, and showing compassion and understanding toward others' emotions and needs. Empathetic individuals can build strong interpersonal connections, resolve conflicts peacefully, and demonstrate genuine care and concern for others.

Empathy, the ability to understand and share the feelings of others, is a concept that resonates throughout the Bible. However, the term itself might not be explicitly mentioned in the King James Version. Here are some passages that convey the essence of empathy:

1. Romans 12:15 - "Rejoice with them that do rejoice, and weep with them that weep." This verse encourages believers to empathize with others by sharing their joys and sorrows, demonstrating compassion and understanding.
2. Galatians 6:2 - "Bear ye one another's burdens, and so fulfill the law of Christ." Here, believers are called to empathize by helping carry each other's burdens, showing support and solidarity in times of need.
3. 1 Corinthians 12:26 - "And whether one member suffers, all the members suffer with it, or one member be honored, all the members rejoice with it." This verse illustrates the interconnectedness of believers in the body of Christ, emphasizing the shared experience of suffering and rejoicing and thereby promoting empathy and compassion among believers
4. Philippians 2:4 - "Look not every man on his own things, but every man also on the things of others." This verse encourages believers to have empathy by

13

considering the needs and concerns of others rather than solely focusing on their own interests.

5. Colossians 3:12 - "Put on therefore, as the elect of God, holy and beloved, bowels of mercies, kindness, humbleness of mind, meekness, longsuffering." This passage encourages believers to clothe themselves with empathy, mercy, and kindness, reflecting the compassionate nature of God in their interactions with others.

While "empathy" may not be explicitly used, these passages convey the biblical principles of understanding, compassion, and solidarity with others, foundational to empathy.

Social Skills: Social skills encompass a range of abilities related to effective communication, collaboration, and relationship-building. This component involves communicating clearly and assertively, working well in teams, resolving conflicts constructively, and building rapport with others. Individuals with strong social skills can build networks, influence others positively, and quickly navigate social situations.

Social skills, which involve effective communication, relationship-building, and interaction with others, are addressed indirectly in several passages throughout the Bible. Here are some verses that touch upon aspects of social skills:

1. Proverbs 18:24 - "A man that hath friends must shew himself friendly: and there is a friend that sticketh closer than a brother." This verse emphasizes the importance of being friendly and approachable in building and maintaining friendships, highlighting the reciprocity of social interactions.

2. Proverbs 15:1 - "A soft answer turneth away wrath: but grievous words stir up anger." This verse speaks to the importance of communication and the impact of our words on others, suggesting that using gentle and respectful language can defuse conflicts and promote positive interactions.

3. Proverbs 16:24 - "Pleasant words are as a honeycomb, sweet to the soul, and health to the bones." Here, the value of kind and pleasant speech is emphasized, highlighting its positive effect on others' well-being and the quality of relationships.

4. Proverbs 22:24-25 - "Make no friendship with an angry man; and with a furious man thou shalt not go: Lest thou learn his ways, and get a snare to thy soul." This passage offers practical advice on choosing social connections wisely, cautioning against associating with those who have negative or harmful behaviors.

5. Ephesians 4:29 - "Let no corrupt communication proceed out of your mouth, but that which is good to the use of edifying, that it may minister grace unto the hearers." This verse instructs believers to use their words to build others up and promote positive interactions rather than engaging in negative or harmful communication.

6. Colossians 4:6 - "Let your speech be alway with grace, seasoned with salt, that ye may know how ye ought to answer every man." This verse encourages believers to communicate with grace and wisdom, adapting their speech to effectively engage with others in various social situations.

While the Bible may not explicitly use "social skills," these passages provide timeless wisdom and guidance for navigating social interactions with wisdom, kindness, and grace.

Overall, emotional intelligence involves a combination of these components, enabling individuals to better understand themselves and others, manage emotions effectively, and build strong and meaningful relationships. Developing emotional intelligence can improve personal and professional success, enhance well-being, and increase overall life satisfaction.

The Significance Of EI In Modern Leadership

Emotional Intelligence (EI) holds significant importance in modern leadership due to its impact on effective communication, relationship-building, decision-making, and overall organizational success. Here are several reasons why EI is crucial in contemporary leadership:

1. Enhanced Communication: Leaders with high EI are adept at recognizing and understanding emotions in themselves and others. This enables them to communicate effectively, empathize with their team members, and tailor their message to resonate with different individuals or groups within the organization.
2. Improved Relationship Building: EI is pivotal in building strong, trusting relationships within teams and across the organization. Emotionally intelligent leaders are better equipped to establish rapport, foster collaboration, and constructively resolve conflicts, leading to higher engagement and productivity among team members.
3. Better Decision-Making: Leaders with high EI can regulate their emotions and remain composed even in high-pressure situations. This allows them to make sound, rational decisions based on objective analysis rather than being swayed by emotions. Additionally, EI enables leaders to consider their decisions' impact

16

on others and consider their perspectives, leading to more inclusive and effective decision-making processes.

4. Increased Adaptability: Adaptability is essential for leadership success in today's rapidly changing business environment. Leaders with high EI are more flexible and resilient in the face of challenges and uncertainties, as they can manage their emotions, remain open to feedback, and adapt their approach as needed to navigate complex situations.

5. Enhanced Employee Engagement and Retention: Leaders who demonstrate empathy, authenticity, and emotional intelligence are more likely to inspire trust and loyalty among their team members. Employees feel valued, understood, and supported by emotionally intelligent leaders, leading to higher job satisfaction, engagement, and retention within the organization.

6. Positive Organizational Culture: EI not only impacts individual leadership effectiveness but also contributes to the overall organizational culture. Leaders who prioritize EI create a culture of psychological safety where employees feel comfortable expressing themselves, taking risks, and innovating without fear of judgment or retribution. This fosters employee creativity, collaboration, and a sense of belonging, driving organizational success.

In summary, EI is indispensable in modern leadership as it fosters effective communication, relationship-building, decision-making, adaptability, employee engagement, and positive organizational culture. Leaders who cultivate emotional intelligence skills are better equipped to navigate the complexities of the modern business landscape and drive sustainable success for their organizations.

Below are three examples of a lack of Emotional Intelligence. These examples highlight the importance of emotional intelligence in navigating interpersonal relationships, managing conflict, and making sound decisions in alignment with God's will.

1. Saul's Jealousy Towards David (1 Samuel 18:6-9):

In the book of 1 Samuel, we see King Saul's inability to manage his emotions effectively when David, a young shepherd, gained popularity after defeating Goliath. Instead of celebrating David's victory and embracing him as an asset to the kingdom, Saul's jealousy and insecurity consumed him. He became increasingly hostile towards David, even attempting to kill him multiple times. This lack of emotional intelligence led to Saul making irrational decisions driven by envy and fear, ultimately leading to his downfall.

2. Peter's Denial of Jesus (Matthew 26:69-75):

In the New Testament, during Jesus' trial and crucifixion, Peter, one of Jesus' closest disciples, demonstrated a lack of emotional intelligence when he denied knowing Jesus three times. Despite his earlier bravado and declarations of loyalty to Jesus, Peter succumbed to fear and self-preservation when faced with the pressure of the situation. His inability to manage his emotions, particularly his fear of persecution, led to actions that contradicted his professed beliefs and caused him deep remorse afterward.

3. Jonah's Anger Towards Nineveh (Jonah 4:1-4):

The story of Jonah illustrates another example of emotional immaturity in the Bible. After reluctantly obeying God's command to preach repentance to the people of Nineveh, Jonah became angry when they repented, and God showed them mercy. Jonah's emotional response reveals his lack of empathy and compassion for the people of Nineveh and his inability to understand God's overarching plan for redemption. His anger and resentment blinded him to the bigger picture, causing him to focus only on his own desires and discomfort.

The Connection Between Emotional Intelligence And Effective Leadership

The connection between emotional intelligence (EI) and effective Christian leadership is profound, as both concepts emphasize the importance of understanding and managing emotions, fostering strong relationships, and serving others with humility and compassion. Emotional Intelligence contributes to effective Christian leadership in four ways:

1. Understanding Emotions
2. Empathy and Compassion
3. Building Strong Relationships
4. Servant Leadership

1. **Understanding Emotions:** Effective Christian leaders must understand their own emotions and the emotions of those they lead. This self-awareness, a key component of EI, enables leaders to recognize how their feelings influence their thoughts, behaviors, and interactions with others. Understanding their emotional triggers and responses, Christian leaders can maintain composure, make sound decisions, and lead authentically and honestly.

Question	Response
1. How do my emotions impact my leadership style and effectiveness in guiding others within a Christian context?	
2. What specific instances have I observed my emotions influencing my thoughts, actions, or decision-making processes as a Christian leader?	
3. Can I identify recurring emotional triggers that tend to affect my leadership negatively or positively, and how do I manage them?	
4. In what ways have I demonstrated self-awareness in understanding my emotional responses in various leadership situations?	
5. How do I ensure that my emotional responses align with the values and principles of Christian	

leadership, such as compassion, forgiveness, and empathy?	
6. Have I actively sought feedback or insights from others about how my emotions impact our interactions and the overall dynamics within the leadership environment?	
7. Reflecting on past experiences, how have I handled moments of emotional turmoil or conflict as a Christian leader, and what lessons have I learned from those experiences?	
8. How do I balance the need for authenticity in expressing my emotions while maintaining professionalism and integrity in my leadership role?	
9. Have there been times when I have consciously used my understanding of emotions to positively influence the emotional	

climate and morale within my team or organization?	
10. What steps am I currently taking to further develop my emotional intelligence as a Christian leader, and how do I plan to integrate these insights into my leadership approach moving forward?	

2. **Empathy and Compassion:** EI emphasizes empathy and compassion toward others, which is central to Christian leadership. Jesus Christ exemplified empathy by understanding and ministering to the needs of others, regardless of their background or circumstances. Christian leaders with high levels of empathy can connect with their team members on a deeper level, demonstrate genuine care and concern, and foster a culture of support and understanding within their organizations.

Question	Response
1. How do I actively demonstrate empathy and compassion in my interactions with others, both within and outside my leadership role?	
2. Reflecting on the example of Jesus Christ, how do I strive to understand and minister to the needs of those I lead, regardless of their background or circumstances?	
3. Can I recall specific instances where I have effectively connected with team members on a deeper level through empathy, and what were the outcomes of those interactions?	
4. How do I cultivate a culture of support and understanding within my organization by embodying empathy and compassion as a Christian leader?	

5. Have there been times when I've struggled to empathize with certain individuals or situations, and what strategies do I employ to overcome these challenges?	
6. How do I balance empathy with accountability and decision-making in my leadership approach, ensuring compassion and effectiveness?	
7. Do I actively seek opportunities to listen and understand the perspectives and experiences of others, particularly those who may be marginalized or overlooked?	
8. How do I integrate empathy into my leadership practices to foster team cohesion, trust, and collaboration?	
9. How do I navigate situations where empathy may conflict with organizational goals or objectives, and	

how do I reconcile these tensions as a Christian leader?	
10. What steps am I taking to continually develop and deepen my capacity for empathy and compassion in my leadership journey?	

3. **Building Strong Relationships:** Effective Christian leadership is built on solid and meaningful relationships with others. EI equips leaders with the social skills to build rapport, communicate effectively, and resolve conflicts peacefully. By investing in relationships based on trust, respect, and mutual understanding, Christian leaders can create a sense of community and belonging within their teams, fostering collaboration and unity.

Examples from Scripture:

- Building Rapport and Trust:

"A man that hath friends must shew himself friendly: and there is a friend that sticketh closer than a brother." Proverbs 18:24

- Effective Communication:

"Let your speech be alway with grace, seasoned with salt, that ye may know how ye ought to answer every man." Colossians 4:6

- Resolving Conflicts Peacefully:

"Blessed are the peacemakers: for they shall be called the children of God." Matthew 5:9

- Fostering Collaboration and Unity:

"Endeavouring to keep the unity of the Spirit in the bond of peace." Ephesians 4:3

- Investing in Relationships:

"Bear ye one another's burdens, and so fulfill the law of Christ." Galatians 6:2

- Creating a Sense of Community and Belonging:

"For where two or three are gathered together in my name, there am I in the midst of them."

Matthew 18:20

- Mutual Understanding:

"So we, being many, are one body in Christ, and every one member one of another." Romans 12:5

- Demonstrating Respect:

"Let nothing be done through strife or vainglory, but in lowliness of mind let each esteem other better than themselves." Philippians 2:3

- Encouraging Collaboration:

"Two are better than one because they have a good reward for their labor." Ecclesiastes 4:9

- Nurturing Community:

"And they continued steadfastly in the apostles' doctrine and fellowship, and in breaking of bread, and in prayers." Acts 2:42

Question`	Response
1. How do I prioritize building strong and meaningful relationships with those I lead in alignment with the principles of Christian leadership?	
2. Reflecting on my current leadership approach, how effectively do I utilize emotional intelligence to build rapport and establish trust within my team?	
3. Can I recall instances where I've successfully resolved conflicts peacefully by applying social skills and emotional intelligence in my leadership role?	
4. How do I actively invest in relationships based on trust, respect, and mutual	

understanding within my team or organization?	
5. How do I foster a sense of community and belonging among team members, ensuring everyone feels valued and included in our mission as Christian leaders?	
6. Do I regularly seek feedback from team members to gauge the strength of our relationships and identify areas for improvement in fostering collaboration and unity?	
7. How do I demonstrate genuine care and concern for the well-being of those I lead, beyond professional responsibilities, to deepen our connections and relationships?	
8. Have there been instances where I've faced challenges in building relationships within my team, and	

what strategies have I employed to overcome these obstacles?	
9. How do I model trust, respect, and mutual understanding in my interactions with others, setting a positive example for the team to follow in our pursuit of Christian leadership values?	
10. What steps am I currently taking to further develop my social skills and emotional intelligence as a Christian leader to enhance my ability to build and maintain strong relationships with those around me?	

4. **Servant Leadership:** At the heart of Christian leadership is the concept of servant leadership, where leaders prioritize serving others above self-interest. EI aligns with this leadership model by encouraging leaders to put the needs of their team members first, lead with humility, and empower others to succeed. Servant leaders with high EI can listen attentively, provide support and guidance, and

create opportunities for growth and development among their followers.

Question	Response
1. How do I personally embody the principles of servant leadership in my role as a Christian leader, prioritizing the needs and well-being of others above my own interests?	
2. Reflecting on my leadership journey, how have I demonstrated humility in my interactions with those I lead, and how has this impacted the dynamics within my team or organization?	
3. Can I identify specific instances where my emotional intelligence has enabled me to effectively listen to the concerns and aspirations of my team members, and how did I respond to their needs?	

4. How do I empower and support the growth and development of others within my sphere of influence as a servant leader with high emotional intelligence?	
5. How do I balance the responsibility of leading with humility and serving others with the necessity of making tough decisions and providing direction in my leadership role?	
6. Have there been times when I've struggled to prioritize the needs of others over my own self-interests, and what strategies do I employ to realign with the principles of servant leadership?	
7. Do I actively seek feedback from team members to assess whether I am effectively serving their needs and fostering an environment of	

empowerment and growth?	
8. How do I create opportunities for individuals to thrive and excel within their roles, leveraging my emotional intelligence to understand their strengths, weaknesses, and aspirations?	
9. Have there been moments when I've encountered resistance or skepticism towards servant leadership, and how do I navigate these challenges while remaining true to my values and principles?	
10. What steps am I taking to further develop my emotional intelligence and deepen my commitment to servant leadership to better serve and support those entrusted to my care?	

5. **Forgiveness and Grace:** Christianity emphasizes forgiveness and grace towards others, even in the face of adversity. Leaders with high EI understand

the importance of forgiveness towards themselves and others, allowing for reconciliation and healing within their teams. Christian leaders can cultivate a culture of trust, resilience, and unity by extending grace and offering second chances, enabling their organizations to thrive even in challenging times.

Question	Response
1. How do I personally integrate the principles of forgiveness and grace into my leadership approach, particularly when faced with challenging or adverse situations within my team or organization?	
2. Reflecting on past experiences, can I recall instances where practicing forgiveness, whether towards myself or others, has led to reconciliation and healing, positively impacting the overall dynamics within my team?	
3. How do I demonstrate empathy and understanding towards	

those who may have made mistakes or faced setbacks, fostering an environment of compassion and support within my leadership sphere?	
4. How do I balance the need for accountability and responsibility with offering second chances and extending grace to individuals within my team or organization?	
5. Can I identify any biases or personal barriers that may hinder my ability to forgive or extend grace to others, and what steps am I taking to overcome these obstacles in my leadership journey?	
6. Have there been moments when I've struggled to forgive myself or others for past actions or decisions, and how do I navigate these challenges while maintaining integrity and authenticity in my leadership role?	

7. Do I actively encourage open dialogue and communication within my team, creating a safe space for individuals to express remorse, seek forgiveness, and work toward reconciliation?	
8. How do I foster a culture of trust and resilience within my organization by exemplifying forgiveness and grace in my interactions with colleagues, subordinates, and peers?	
9. Have there been instances where forgiveness has led to unexpected positive outcomes or strengthened relationships within my leadership sphere, and what lessons have I learned from these experiences?	
10. What strategies am I implementing to further develop my emotional intelligence and deepen my understanding of forgiveness and grace as	

essential components of effective leadership in a Christian context?	

The connection between emotional intelligence and effective Christian leadership lies in their shared values of empathy, compassion, humility, and service. By integrating EI principles into their leadership approach, Christian leaders can inspire and empower their teams to fulfill their mission, positively impact their communities, and, ultimately, glorify God through their leadership endeavors.

Chapter Two:
Understanding Christian Leadership

Values and principles are paramount in guiding leadership behaviors and decisions, as they are the foundation for effective leadership. Here's a comprehensive discussion of their importance:

1. **Alignment with Organizational Culture:** Values and principles help leaders align their actions with the organization's overall culture. When leaders embody and uphold the organization's core values, they contribute to a cohesive and unified work environment.

2. **Ethical Decision Making:** Values and principles provide a moral compass for leaders, guiding them in making ethical decisions. In today's complex business landscape, ethical leadership is crucial for building trust and credibility with stakeholders, including employees, customers, and the community.

3. **Building Trust and Credibility:** Leaders who consistently adhere to values and principles earn the trust and respect of their team members. When employees see their leaders acting with integrity and transparency, they are more likely to trust their decisions and follow their lead.

4. **Setting a Positive Example:** Leaders serve as role models for their teams, and their actions speak louder than words. By embodying values such as honesty, accountability, and respect, leaders set a positive example for others to emulate, fostering a culture of integrity and excellence.

5. **Effective Decision Making**: Values and principles serve as guiding principles in decision-making processes. When faced with tough choices, leaders can

refer to their core values to ensure their decisions align with the organization's mission and vision.

6. **Driving Organizational Performance:** Leaders who prioritize values and principles tend to create high-performing teams. When employees feel valued, respected, and aligned with the organization's values, they are more motivated and engaged, leading to improved productivity and performance.

7. **Resolving Ethical Dilemmas:** In challenging situations where ethical dilemmas arise, values and principles provide a framework for leaders to navigate complex issues. By prioritizing principles such as fairness, justice, and integrity, leaders can make decisions that uphold the organization's reputation and long-term success.

8. **Crisis Management and Resilience:** During times of crisis or uncertainty, values and principles serve as a stabilizing force for leaders and their teams. By staying true to their core values, leaders can inspire confidence, foster resilience, and guide their organizations through turbulent times with integrity and resolve.

In conclusion, values and principles are essential pillars of effective leadership, guiding behaviors and decisions in alignment with organizational goals, ethical standards, and the well-being of stakeholders. By embodying and upholding these principles, leaders can create a culture of trust, integrity, and excellence, driving sustainable success for their organizations.

Leadership In A Christian Context

Leadership in a Christian context is distinguished by its foundation in specific principles and values derived from the teachings of Jesus Christ. As followers of Christ, Christian leaders are called to embody these timeless ideals in their leadership practices, guiding their interactions, decisions, and relationships with humility, compassion, and integrity.

1. Humility:

At the heart of Christian leadership is humility, modeled after the example set by Jesus Christ himself. Humility involves a recognition of one's own limitations and a willingness to serve others selflessly without seeking recognition or status.

In Philippians 2:3-4, Christian leaders are called to "do nothing out of selfish ambition or vain conceit, but in humility consider others better than yourselves. Each of you should look not only to your own interests but also to the interests of others."

By humbly acknowledging their dependence on God and interconnectedness with others, Christian leaders create environments of trust, respect, and collaboration where individuals can flourish and contribute their unique gifts and talents.

2. Servant Leadership:

Christian leadership is characterized by servant leadership, a model exemplified by Jesus Christ, who declared, "For even the Son of Man did not come to be served, but to serve, and to give his life as a ransom for many" (Mark 10:45).

Servant leaders prioritize the needs of others above their own, seeking to empower and uplift those they lead. They lead with humility, empathy, and compassion, serving as stewards of God's resources and shepherds of His people.

Christian leaders inspire and empower others to reach their full potential by cultivating a servant-hearted approach to leadership and fostering a culture of service, teamwork, and mutual support.

3. Love:

Central to Christian leadership is the principle of love, encapsulated in Jesus Christ's commandment to "love your neighbor as yourself" (Matthew 22:39). Love is the foundational principle that guides all aspects of leadership, shaping how leaders interact with their followers, colleagues, and stakeholders.

Christian leaders demonstrate love through acts of kindness, generosity, and forgiveness, seeking the well-being and flourishing of all individuals under their care. Love transcends race, ethnicity, and background boundaries, uniting diverse communities in unity, compassion, and grace.

4. Empathy:

Empathy is a cornerstone of Christian leadership, reflecting Jesus Christ's ability to "empathize with our weaknesses" (Hebrews 4:15). Christian leaders strive to understand and share in the experiences, emotions, and perspectives of those they lead, fostering deeper connections and meaningful relationships. By practicing empathy, leaders demonstrate care and concern for the holistic well-being of their followers, creating a culture of compassion, understanding, and mutual support.

In summary, leadership in a Christian context is rooted in humility, servant leadership, love, and empathy—timeless principles and values derived from the teachings of Jesus Christ. By embodying these ideals, Christian leaders inspire and empower others to pursue excellence, justice, and righteousness, ultimately reflecting the transformative power of God's love in the world.

Empowering Leadership

Empowerment refers to enabling individuals or groups to gain control over their lives, make informed decisions, and take action to achieve their goals and aspirations. It involves providing people with the resources, skills, knowledge, and opportunities necessary to realize their full potential and participate actively in society.

At its core, empowerment fosters autonomy, agency, and self-determination. It is not merely about granting power or authority to others but rather about facilitating individuals' ability to assert their rights, advocate for their needs, and contribute meaningfully to their communities. Empowerment recognizes every person's inherent dignity and worth and seeks to remove barriers that inhibit their ability to thrive.

Key components of empowering leadership include:

1. **Trust and Support**: Empowering leaders trust their team members and provide them with the support and resources needed to succeed. They believe in the capabilities of their followers and create a supportive environment where individuals feel valued and encouraged to take risks and innovate.

2. **Delegation of Authority:** Empowering leaders delegate responsibility and decision-making authority to their team members, giving them a sense of ownership and accountability for their work. By empowering others to make decisions, leaders enable individuals to develop their skills and confidence.

3. **Encouragement of Autonomy:** Empowering leaders promote autonomy by giving individuals the freedom to exercise their judgment and creativity in accomplishing tasks and solving problems. They provide guidance and direction

when needed, allowing room for experimentation and learning from mistakes.

4. **Development of Potential:** Empowering leaders invest in the growth and development of their followers. They provide training, mentoring, and skill-building opportunities, helping individuals reach their full potential and advance in their careers. Empowering leaders also recognize and celebrate the achievements and contributions of their team members.

5. **Inspirational Communication:** Empowering leaders inspire and motivate their followers through clear communication, vision, and enthusiasm. They articulate a compelling vision for the future and communicate how everyone's contributions contribute to the organization's larger goals. Empowering leaders also actively listen to the ideas and concerns of their team members, fostering open and honest communication.

Overall, empowering leadership creates a culture of empowerment where individuals feel valued, motivated, and engaged. By empowering their followers, leaders can unleash the full potential of their teams, foster innovation and creativity, and drive organizational success in a rapidly changing and complex world.

The Connection of emotional intelligence with empowering leadership, grounded in Christian values and principles, creates a dynamic framework for compassionate and effective leadership. At its core, emotional intelligence emphasizes self-awareness, self-regulation, empathy, and social skills, all of which are essential qualities for empowering leaders. By understanding and managing their emotions, empowering leaders can cultivate inner peace and stability, enabling them to lead with clarity and authenticity.

Emotional Intelligence enables leaders to empathize with the experiences and perspectives of their followers, fostering a culture of trust, respect, and collaboration. Empowering leaders recognize each individual's inherent dignity and worth, reflecting the Christian principle of loving one's neighbor as oneself. This empathy extends beyond mere understanding to active compassion and support for the well-being and growth of others.

In the context of Christian values and principles, empowering leadership is rooted in the example of Jesus Christ, who demonstrated humility, servant leadership, and sacrificial love. Jesus taught his disciples to serve others humbly and empower them to fulfill their potential. Similarly, empowering leaders lead by example, serving as mentors and role models who empower others to excel and thrive.

The connection also involves aligning leadership practices with biblical justice, mercy, and stewardship teachings. Empowering leaders seek to create inclusive and equitable environments where all individuals are valued and supported, regardless of their background or circumstances. They prioritize the well-being of their team members and strive to foster a sense of belonging and purpose within the organization.

Furthermore, empowering leadership grounded in Christian values emphasizes the importance of ethical conduct, integrity, and servant leadership. Leaders are called to prioritize the needs of others above their own and to use their authority and influence to serve the greater good.

By embodying the virtues of humility, compassion, and grace, empowering leaders inspire and empower others to reach their full potential, ultimately contributing to the flourishing of individuals, organizations, and communities.

A Christian Approach to Emotional Intelligence presents several challenging aspects that leaders may encounter as they strive to integrate Emotional Intelligence with Christian principles in their leadership approach. One of the most challenging aspects is navigating the tension between assertiveness and humility.

Navigating the tension between assertiveness and humility while integrating emotional intelligence, Christian values, and principles can be a complex yet rewarding endeavor. Here are several strategies to overcome this challenge:

First, developing a deep understanding of assertiveness and humility within emotional intelligence and Christian teachings is crucial. Assertiveness, when rooted in emotional intelligence, involves expressing one's needs and opinions respectfully while considering the feelings and perspectives of others. Humility, however, entails recognizing one's strengths without boasting and being open to learning from others.

One approach is cultivating self-awareness, a cornerstone of emotional intelligence and Christian spirituality. Reflect on your own tendencies towards assertiveness and humility. Are there situations where you struggle to find the balance? By understanding your own inclinations, you can consciously work towards aligning your actions with Christian values of compassion, empathy, and selflessness.

The second strategy is to practice active listening and empathy. When interacting with others, strive to genuinely understand their perspectives and feelings. This requires setting aside your ego and embracing humility. By listening attentively and empathizing with others' experiences, you can respond assertively while still honoring their dignity and worth as fellow individuals created in the image of God.

Intentionally seek feedback from trusted mentors, peers, or spiritual guides. Constructive feedback can provide valuable insights into how your assertiveness and humility are perceived by others. Be open to receiving feedback with humility, recognizing that growth often requires acknowledging areas for improvement.

Furthermore, integrate prayer and spiritual reflection into your journey of balancing assertiveness and humility. Seek guidance from God through prayer, meditation, and studying scriptures. Allow the wisdom of Christian teachings to inform your decisions and actions, guiding you toward a more harmonious integration of assertiveness and humility in your interactions.

Last, remember that achieving balance is a continual process rather than a destination. Embrace the journey of growth and learning, knowing that setbacks and challenges are opportunities for deeper self-awareness and spiritual transformation. By staying committed to integrating emotional intelligence with Christian values, you can navigate the tension between assertiveness and humility with grace and authenticity.

While effective leadership requires assertiveness in decision-making and goal-setting, Christian values emphasize humility and servant leadership. Balancing these qualities can be challenging, as leaders must assert themselves confidently while remaining humble and open to feedback and collaboration.

Another challenging aspect is managing conflict in a Christian manner. Conflict is inevitable in any organization, but it can be difficult to resolve it in a way that honors Christian values such as forgiveness, reconciliation, and love. Leaders must navigate conflicts with grace and compassion, seeking solutions that effectively promote understanding and unity while addressing underlying issues.

Additionally, maintaining authenticity and integrity in leadership can be challenging, especially in environments where there may be pressure to compromise one's values for expediency or success. Leaders must stay true to their Christian principles and values, even when faced with difficult decisions or temptations to stray from their moral compass.

Fostering inclusivity and diversity within the organization while upholding Christian values can present challenges. Leaders must ensure that everyone feels valued, respected, and included, regardless of their background, beliefs, or identity. This requires creating a culture of acceptance and belonging where differences are celebrated and leveraged for the organization's benefit.

A Christian Approach to Emotional Intelligence offers a transformative approach to leadership, it also presents challenges that require leaders to navigate with wisdom, humility, and grace.

By embracing these challenges and striving to integrate Emotional Intelligence with Christian values in their leadership approach, leaders can foster a culture of compassion, collaboration, and excellence that empowers individuals and transforms organizations for the better.

How To Overcome Obstacles And Stay Focused On Long-Term Objectives Through Emotional Intelligence

Understanding how to overcome obstacles and stay focused on long-term objectives through emotional intelligence (EI) and Christian values involves several key principles and practices.

First and foremost, individuals must cultivate self-awareness, recognizing their emotions, strengths, and weaknesses. By understanding their emotional responses to challenges, individuals can better regulate their emotions and maintain a positive mindset, even in adversity.

Additionally, individuals can draw on Christian values such as faith, resilience, and perseverance to overcome obstacles. By trusting in God's guidance and provision, individuals can find strength and hope in difficult times, knowing they are not alone in their struggles. Through prayer, meditation, and reflection on biblical teachings, individuals can find solace and inspiration to persevere in pursuing their long-term objectives.

Individuals can leverage empathy and social skills to seek support and collaboration from others. By fostering strong relationships and networks, individuals can gain valuable insights, resources, and encouragement to overcome obstacles and achieve their goals.

Additionally, by demonstrating empathy and compassion towards others, individuals can build trust and rapport, creating a supportive community that uplifts and empowers one another. Moreover, individuals can stay focused on long-term objectives by setting SMART goals (Specific, Measurable,

Achievable, Relevant, and Time-bound) and developing a clear action plan to achieve them.

Individuals can maintain momentum and track progress by breaking down long-term objectives into smaller, manageable tasks. Additionally, individuals can regularly reassess their goals and adjust their strategies as needed, remaining flexible and adaptable in changing circumstances.

Overall, understanding how to overcome obstacles and stay focused on long-term objectives through EI and Christian values involves a holistic approach that integrates self-awareness, faith, empathy, and strategic planning. By cultivating these qualities and practices, individuals can navigate challenges with resilience, perseverance, and grace, ultimately achieving their goals and fulfilling their purpose in life.

Daily Life

Mastering emotional intelligence and integrating Christian values and principles into daily life requires a multifaceted approach encompassing self-awareness, self-regulation, empathy, social skills, and a deep understanding of biblical teachings.

To begin, one must cultivate self-awareness by reflecting on their thoughts, feelings, and behaviors in light of Christian values such as love, forgiveness, and compassion. This introspection allows individuals to recognize their strengths and weaknesses, enabling them to align their actions with their faith. In addition, this introspection allows individuals to identify patterns and triggers, empowering them to respond to situations more intentionally rather than reactively.

Self-regulation involves exercising control over one's emotions and impulses, guided by principles of patience, kindness, and self-discipline found in Christian teachings. Through prayer, meditation, and mindfulness, individuals can develop the inner strength necessary to respond to life's challenges with grace and humility.

Moreover, mastering emotional intelligence entails developing empathy, which is the ability to understand and share the feelings of others. In the context of Christian values, empathy is rooted in the commandment to love one's neighbor as oneself, fostering a genuine concern for the well-being of others.

By actively listening, showing compassion, and offering support to those in need, individuals can build meaningful connections and contribute to a more compassionate and harmonious society.

Furthermore, honing social skills involves effectively navigating interpersonal relationships while upholding Christian virtues such as honesty, integrity, and respect. Cultivating a spirit of cooperation, collaboration, and teamwork fosters a sense of community grounded in mutual respect and understanding.

Integrating Christian values and principles into daily life also requires a deep understanding of biblical teachings and a commitment to living according to God's word. Regular study of scripture, participation in worship and fellowship, and engagement in acts of service and charity are essential components of a life lived under Christian values.

By grounding oneself in the teachings of Jesus Christ and seeking to emulate His example of love, compassion, and humility, individuals can cultivate a more meaningful and fulfilling existence.

Ultimately, mastering emotional intelligence and embracing Christian values and principles in daily life is a lifelong journey that requires dedication, self-reflection, and a willingness to grow spiritually and emotionally. Through steadfast faith, prayerful discernment, and a commitment to living with integrity and compassion, individuals can experience greater harmony, purpose, and purpose fulfillment.

Question	Response
1. Reflect on a time when you witnessed a leader embodying values and principles effectively. How did their actions impact the organization or team?	
2. Consider a challenging decision you've had to make recently. How did your values and principles influence your decision-making process?	
3. How do you think integrating values and principles into leadership practices can build trust and	

credibility within an organization or team?	
4. Reflect on the role of humility in leadership, as discussed in the Christian context. How do you perceive humility influencing effective leadership?	
5. Think about a leader you admire, whether from a religious or secular context. What qualities or values do they possess that you find particularly inspiring or influential?	
6. In what ways do you believe empathy enhances leadership effectiveness, as highlighted in both the general and Christian leadership contexts? Can you provide examples from your experiences where empathy was pivotal in leadership dynamics?	
7. How do you perceive the concept of empowerment, as	

described in the provided text? Reflect on instances in your life where you felt empowered or empowered others. What factors contributed to this feeling of empowerment?	
8. Consider the key components of empowering leadership outlined in the text. Which component resonates with you the most, and why? How do you envision incorporating this component into your own leadership style or practices?	
9. Reflect on the intersection of emotional intelligence and empowering leadership within a Christian context. How do you think emotional intelligence can enhance the effectiveness of empowering leadership, particularly when grounded in Christian values and principles?	

10. Navigating the tension between assertiveness and humility is a challenging aspect of integrating emotional intelligence with Christian principles in leadership. How do you personally approach this balance in your own leadership endeavors? Can you share strategies or experiences that helped you navigate this tension?	
11. Conflict management is another challenging aspect of leadership within a Christian framework. How do you believe Christian values such as forgiveness, reconciliation, and love can inform how leaders approach and resolve conflicts in organizational settings? Can you provide examples or scenarios where you've witnessed or experienced conflict resolution guided by Christian principles?	
12. Reflect on a time when you faced a challenge or obstacle in your personal	

or professional life. How did you apply emotional intelligence and Christian values to overcome this challenge? What lessons did you learn from this experience?	
13. Consider the importance of maintaining authenticity and integrity in leadership, especially when facing pressure to compromise values for success. How do you personally ensure that you stay true to your Christian principles in challenging situations?	
14. Fostering inclusivity and diversity within an organization while upholding Christian values can be challenging. Reflect on ways you've witnessed or experienced leaders successfully navigating this challenge. What strategies or approaches do you believe are effective in creating a culture of acceptance and belonging?	

15. Explore the connection between mastering emotional intelligence and integrating Christian values into daily life. How do you cultivate self-awareness, self-regulation, empathy, and social skills in alignment with Christian principles in your everyday interactions?	
16. The provided text discusses the importance of setting SMART goals and developing a clear action plan to stay focused on long-term objectives. Reflect on a personal or professional goal you've achieved or are currently working towards. How have emotional intelligence and Christian values guided your approach to goal-setting and execution?	

Chapter Three:
Integrating Christian Values Into Emotional Intelligence

Practical Ways To Incorporate Christian Values Into The Development Of Emotional Intelligence

Emotional intelligence (EI) is the ability to understand and manage one's emotions and empathize with and relate to the feelings of others. It is crucial in personal and professional success, influencing relationships, decision-making, and overall well-being.

Integrating Christian values into the development of emotional intelligence offers a unique perspective, emphasizing virtues such as love, empathy, humility, forgiveness, and compassion. This discussion will explore practical ways to incorporate Christian values into cultivating emotional intelligence.

1. Cultivating Self-Awareness:

We encounter various practices deeply rooted in Christian tradition and values in cultivating self-awareness. Firstly, prayer and reflection serve as foundational pillars, guiding individuals to delve into their innermost thoughts, emotions, and behaviors. Through intentional prayer and quiet contemplation, individuals are invited to connect with their spiritual selves, fostering a heightened awareness of their inner landscape.

Secondly, examining conscience, drawn from Christian traditions, offers a structured approach to self-reflection. By evaluating their actions and motivations against moral principles, individuals are prompted to confront areas of growth and development, ultimately leading to increased self-awareness and personal accountability.

Lastly, gratitude journaling is a powerful tool aligned with Christian teachings on thankfulness and contentment. Individuals cultivate a positive mindset and emotional equilibrium by actively recording moments of gratitude and appreciation, enhancing their overall well-being. Together, these practices form a holistic approach to self-awareness, empowering individuals to navigate their inner world with clarity, authenticity, and grace.

2. Developing Empathy:

In the realm of leadership development, the principles of servant leadership, inspired by the example of Jesus Christ, stand as guiding beacons. This approach emphasizes empathy, compassion, and a commitment to prioritizing the needs of others above oneself. By incorporating the tenets of servant leadership into leadership development initiatives, individuals are nurtured in their capacity to understand and support others with genuine care and humility.

Additionally, adhering to the Golden Rule, espoused in Matthew 7:12, emerges as a foundational principle in fostering empathetic and compassionate interactions. Encouraging individuals to treat others with the same kindness and respect they desire for themselves cultivates a culture of empathy and understanding in all interpersonal dealings.

Furthermore, providing opportunities for volunteerism and service offers individuals a tangible way to embody the spirit of servant leadership. Through active engagement in acts of service and volunteering, individuals can walk alongside those in need, gaining firsthand insight into their experiences and fostering a more profound sense of empathy and compassion.

Together, these practices serve not only to shape individuals into empathetic and compassionate leaders but also to nurture a culture of servant leadership that transcends organizational boundaries and fosters a positive impact within communities and beyond.

3. Managing Emotions:

Within emotional intelligence training, incorporating forgiveness practices is a powerful tool for personal growth and healing. Rooted in Christian values, forgiveness is a fundamental principle, urging individuals to release resentment and anger.

By integrating forgiveness practices into emotional intelligence training, individuals can embark on a journey of emotional healing and resilience. Furthermore, biblical meditation offers a profound avenue for reflection and introspection.

Delving into scripture passages that speak to the intricacies of emotions and forgiveness provides practical insights and coping strategies for navigating challenging emotional terrain. Through the lens of Christian teachings, individuals are equipped with the spiritual and emotional tools necessary to confront and overcome obstacles on their journey toward healing and wholeness.

Additionally, the importance of community support cannot be overstated. Christian-based support groups are invaluable resources, offering a sense of belonging and connection within a nurturing environment. These groups provide a safe space for individuals to express their emotions, seek guidance, and receive support from like-minded individuals who share in their journey of faith and emotional growth.

Together, forgiveness practices, biblical meditation, and community support groups form a holistic framework for emotional healing and resilience, empowering individuals to embrace the fullness of their emotions and experience profound transformation in their lives.

4. Building Healthy Relationships:

In the pursuit of building healthy relationships, we find invaluable guidance within the timeless wisdom of Christian teachings. Firstly, integrating biblical communication principles is a cornerstone for fostering deep and meaningful connections. Drawing from passages such as Ephesians 4:15, which exhorts believers to speak truth in love, individuals are equipped with practical insights into effective communication.

By embodying these principles, interpersonal relationships are enriched, and a culture of understanding and empathy is cultivated. Moreover, conflict resolution takes on a transformative dimension when guided by Christian values of love and reconciliation. Encouraging individuals to approach conflicts with humility and a commitment to mutual understanding fosters healthy resolution and strengthens the bonds of trust and respect.

Finally, establishing accountability partnerships within Christian communities offers a supportive personal and relational growth framework. By joining together in mutual accountability, individuals are encouraged to uphold honesty, integrity, and emotional intelligence, nurturing a culture of transparency and growth.

Together, these practices serve as pillars for building healthy relationships grounded in the Christian community's principles of love, grace, and mutual support.

5. Leading by Example:

Leading by example encompasses various facets crucial for effective leadership, among which authentic leadership stands out prominently. Authentic leadership underscores the paramount importance of aligning words with actions. It emphasizes the need for leaders to model integrity and transparency consistently.

Authentic leaders strive to uphold their values and principles in their behavior, fostering trust and respect within their teams and organizations. By demonstrating authenticity, leaders inspire others to do the same, creating a culture of honesty and accountability.

6. Mentorship and Discipleship:

Mentorship and discipleship represent another vital dimension of leading by example, drawing inspiration from the timeless teachings of figures such as Jesus Christ. Encouraging leaders to invest in the development of others mirrors the mentorship and guidance exemplified by Jesus Christ during his earthly ministry.

Just as Jesus mentored his disciples, modern leaders can emulate this approach by nurturing the talents and potential of their team members. Through mentorship, leaders impart knowledge and skills, instill confidence, and empower individuals to reach their full potential.

This commitment to discipleship fosters a culture of continuous learning and growth within organizations, ensuring a legacy of leadership excellence.

In summary, leading by example encompasses authentic leadership and mentorship, both integral to fostering a positive and impactful leadership style. By embodying authenticity and investing in the development of others, leaders can cultivate environments where trust, integrity, and growth thrive.

Drawing insights from exemplary figures like Jesus Christ, leaders can navigate challenges with grace and inspire those around them to strive for excellence in their personal and professional lives.

Conclusion:

Integrating Christian values into the development of emotional intelligence offers a holistic approach that addresses the cognitive aspects of EI and the spiritual and moral dimensions of human flourishing.

Individuals can cultivate emotional intelligence grounded in love, empathy, and Christian virtues by incorporating practices such as prayer, reflection, servant leadership, forgiveness, and biblical guidance.

Ultimately, integrating Christian values enriches emotional intelligence training, leading to more compassionate, resilient, and relationally adept individuals who reflect the character of Christ in their personal and professional lives.

The Role Of Prayer, Reflection, And Spiritual Growth In Enhancing EI From A Christian Standpoint

Amidst the hustle and bustle of leadership, navigating complex emotions and relationships is paramount for success. Emotional intelligence (EI) is crucial in effective leadership, influencing decision-making, communication, and team dynamics.

This book explores the unique intersection of emotional intelligence and Christian spirituality, emphasizing the role of prayer, reflection, and spiritual growth in enhancing EI from a Christian standpoint. Through the lens of faith, senior leaders can deepen their self-awareness, empathy, and resilience, ultimately leading with greater wisdom, compassion, and integrity.

Leading with Prayer and Reflection:

In the journey of leadership, the practice of prayer and reflection stands as a cornerstone of wisdom and discernment. "Leading with Prayer and Reflection" explores the profound impact of prayer in nurturing self-awareness, fostering spiritual growth, and guiding ethical decision-making in senior leadership.

Within the realm of leadership, self-awareness is paramount. Through prayer, leaders embark on a journey of self-discovery, delving into the depths of their hearts and minds to unearth insights into their strengths, weaknesses, and values.

By setting aside time for prayerful introspection, leaders cultivate a heightened awareness of their emotions, motivations, and aspirations, laying a solid foundation for authentic leadership rooted in self-awareness and integrity.

Beyond self-discovery, prayer serves as a conduit for seeking divine wisdom and guidance in leadership. Leaders turn to prayer in moments of uncertainty and decision-making, entrusting their concerns and aspirations to a higher power.

By surrendering to God's will and seeking His guidance through prayer, leaders gain clarity, direction, and discernment, navigating challenges with grace and conviction. In the stillness of prayer, leaders find strength, courage, and assurance, knowing they are not alone in their leadership journey.

In addition to prayer, reflective practices are pivotal in fostering emotional balance and resilience in leadership. "Leading with Prayer and Reflection" introduces leaders to the transformative power of quiet reflection, inviting them to carve out moments of stillness amidst the busyness of their lives.

Through reflection, leaders gain clarity and perspective, discerning the underlying emotions driving their thoughts and actions. By engaging in reflective practices informed by Christian teachings, leaders cultivate emotional intelligence, harnessing their emotions as a source of strength and insight in leadership.

At the heart of "Leading with Prayer and Reflection" lies the imperative of aligning actions with Christian values. Prayer and reflection serve as catalysts for ethical leadership, guiding leaders to uphold principles of honesty, integrity, and compassion in their interactions with others.

Leaders model authentic leadership by grounding their decisions and actions in prayerful discernment and reflection, inspiring trust, respect, and integrity within their organizations and communities.

In conclusion, "Leading with Prayer and Reflection" invites leaders to embark on a transformative prayerful leadership journey rooted in self-awareness, discernment, and integrity. By embracing prayer and reflection as essential practices in leadership, leaders cultivate emotional intelligence, spiritual resilience, and ethical discernment, empowering them to navigate the complexities of leadership with grace, humility, and wisdom.

As leaders embrace the transformative power of prayer and reflection, they embark on a journey of growth, empowerment, and profound impact in their organizations and beyond.

The Power of Prayer in Self-Awareness:

In the intricate tapestry of leadership, self-awareness serves as a guiding light, illuminating the path to authenticity and effectiveness. "The Power of Prayer in Self-Awareness" delves into the transformative role of prayer in self-discovery, unveiling its profound impact on leaders' journey towards deeper understanding and insight.

At the heart of self-awareness lies the willingness to explore the depths of one's inner being. Through prayer, leaders embark on a sacred journey of introspection, peeling back the layers of their souls to uncover the core of their emotions, motivations, and values.

In the silence of prayer, amidst the whispers of the divine, leaders confront their fears, doubts, and insecurities, gaining clarity and perspective on their true selves. By embracing prayer as a vehicle for introspection, leaders cultivate a deeper understanding of themselves, laying the groundwork for authentic and purposeful leadership.

In addition to self-discovery, prayer is a gateway to divine wisdom and guidance in leadership. "The Power of Prayer in Self-Awareness" invites leaders to surrender their concerns and aspirations to a higher power, seeking God's guidance in their decision-making and leadership endeavors.

Through prayerful discernment, leaders align their will with God's, drawing strength and clarity from His infinite wisdom and grace. As they navigate the complexities of leadership, leaders find solace and assurance in the knowledge that they are not alone but accompanied by the guiding hand of the divine.

In the leadership arena, decision-making carries profound implications for the trajectory of organizations and communities. "The Power of Prayer in Self-Awareness" underscores the significance of seeking God's guidance through prayer in decision-making. By surrendering their plans and desires to God, leaders open themselves to divine direction, discerning the path forward with clarity and conviction.

Whether faced with challenges or opportunities, leaders draw upon the wellspring of prayer to navigate with wisdom, humility, and discernment, ensuring that their decisions are aligned with God's will and purpose.

In summary, as leaders embrace "The Power of Prayer in Self-Awareness," they embark on a transformative journey of self-discovery and spiritual growth. Through prayerful introspection and seeking God's guidance, leaders gain insight into their emotions, motivations, and values, paving the way for authentic and purposeful leadership.

By surrendering to the divine and discerning His will in decision-making, leaders navigate the complexities of leadership with grace, humility, and clarity. As they journey deeper into the realms of self-awareness and spiritual enlightenment, leaders become catalysts for transformation, inspiring others to embrace the transformative power of prayer in their own lives and leadership endeavors.

Reflection and Emotional Regulation:

"Reflection and Emotional Regulation" introduces the practice of quiet reflection to manage stress, calm the mind, and foster emotional balance. It encourages leaders to examine their emotions through the lens of Christian teachings, discerning how their beliefs influence their emotional responses.

In the dynamic realm of leadership, finding moments of stillness amidst the chaos is paramount for maintaining emotional balance and clarity of mind. "Reflection and Emotional Regulation" delves into the transformative practice of quiet reflection to manage stress, calm the mind, and foster emotional equilibrium in senior leadership.

Amidst the relentless demands of leadership, carving out moments of silence and solitude becomes an invaluable asset. "Reflection and Emotional Regulation" invites leaders to embrace the practice of quiet reflection, allowing them to withdraw from the noise and distractions of daily life to reconnect with their inner selves.

In the tranquility of reflection, leaders find solace and renewal, replenishing their emotional reserves and gaining clarity of thought amidst the tumultuous currents of leadership. Emotions are an inherent aspect of the human experience, shaping our perceptions, decisions, and interactions with others.

"Reflection and Emotional Regulation" encourages leaders to explore their emotional landscape through the lens of Christian teachings, discerning how their beliefs and values influence their emotional responses. By integrating spiritual insights into their emotional regulation practices, leaders gain a deeper understanding of the underlying motivations and triggers behind their emotions, empowering them to navigate emotional turbulence with grace and resilience.

At the core of "Reflection and Emotional Regulation" lies the imperative of aligning heart and mind in pursuit of emotional balance and harmony. By grounding their reflections in Christian principles of love, compassion, and forgiveness, leaders cultivate a steadfast foundation for emotional regulation rooted in faith and integrity.

Through prayerful introspection and contemplation, leaders harness the transformative power of reflection to cultivate emotional resilience, wisdom, and compassion in their leadership journey.

In summary, as leaders embrace "Reflection and Emotional Regulation," they embark on a transformative journey of self-discovery and emotional mastery. Through quiet reflection and spiritual discernment, leaders learn to navigate the complexities of their emotions with grace, humility, and wisdom.

By integrating Christian teachings into their emotional regulation practices, leaders forge a deeper connection with themselves, others, and the divine, fostering emotional equilibrium and resilience in their leadership endeavors. As they journey toward emotional mastery, leaders become beacons of light and inspiration, illuminating the path for others to follow in their pursuit of emotional balance and spiritual growth.

Spiritual Growth:

The heart of spiritual growth lies in cultivating compassion – a transformative virtue that transcends boundaries and fosters genuine connections with others. "Spiritual Growth and Empathy" delves into how leaders nurture compassion through spiritual practices such as prayer, meditation, and service, embracing every individual's inherent dignity and worth.

By embodying the teachings of Christ on love and compassion, leaders become catalysts for healing and reconciliation in their communities, fostering an atmosphere of empathy and understanding.

Embracing Diversity: The Fruit of Spiritual Maturity

As leaders embark on the journey of spiritual growth, they embrace the rich tapestry of human diversity with openness and acceptance. "Spiritual Growth and Empathy" celebrates the transformative power of spiritual maturity in enabling leaders to appreciate the unique perspectives and experiences of others.

Through the lens of faith, leaders recognize the inherent value of diversity, fostering an inclusive environment where every voice is heard and valued. By embracing diversity, leaders enrich their leadership practices with a breadth of insights and perspectives, strengthening their capacity for empathy and understanding.

Empathy in Action: Bridging the Gulf of Understanding

In leadership, empathy serves as a bridge that spans the gulf of understanding between individuals, fostering meaningful connections built on mutual respect and compassion. "Spiritual Growth and Empathy" explores how leaders embody empathy in their interactions, listening with compassion and seeking to understand the perspectives and experiences of others. Through acts of empathy, leaders cultivate trust, rapport, and collaboration, creating an environment where everyone feels seen, heard, and valued.

In short, as leaders embrace "Spiritual Growth and Empathy," they embark on a transformative journey of compassionate leadership rooted in spiritual maturity and empathy. By nurturing virtues such as compassion and kindness, leaders enrich their leadership practices with depth, authenticity, and humanity.

Through the transformative power of empathy, leaders become beacons of light and compassion, inspiring others to cultivate empathy and understanding in their own lives and leadership endeavors.

As leaders journey towards compassionate leadership, they sow the seeds of healing, reconciliation, and unity in their organizations and communities, leaving a lasting legacy of love and empathy for generations.

Forgiveness and Resilience:

In the realm of leadership, navigating challenges and setbacks with grace and fortitude requires a steadfast commitment to forgiveness and resilience. "Forgiveness and Resilience in Leadership" explores the transformative power of forgiveness in promoting emotional healing, resilience, and reconciliation, drawing inspiration from timeless biblical teachings.

At the heart of "Forgiveness and Resilience in Leadership" lies the recognition of forgiveness as a catalyst for emotional healing and renewal. Through forgiveness, leaders release themselves from the burdens of resentment, anger, and bitterness, experiencing a profound sense of liberation and inner peace.

Drawing upon the teachings of Christ on forgiveness, leaders extend grace and compassion to others, fostering an environment of healing and reconciliation within their organizations and communities. By embracing forgiveness as a cornerstone of leadership, leaders cultivate a culture of empathy, understanding, and restoration, laying the groundwork for resilience in the face of adversity.

Trusting in God's Plan: Fostering Resilience Through Faith

In addition to forgiveness, resilience in leadership is nurtured through unwavering faith in God's sovereignty and providence. It also explores how leaders draw strength and courage from their faith, trusting in God's plan despite trials and tribulations.

By surrendering their fears and anxieties to God, leaders find solace and assurance in His steadfast love and care, empowering them to persevere through adversity with grace and conviction. Through the lens of faith, leaders embrace challenges as opportunities for growth and transformation, emerging from setbacks with renewed vigor and resilience.

As leaders embody forgiveness and resilience in their leadership practices, they become beacons of light and hope in times of adversity. "Forgiveness and Resilience in Leadership" emphasizes the importance of leading gracefully and compassion, extending understanding and support to those who have faltered or failed.

By modeling forgiveness and resilience in their actions, leaders inspire others to embrace the transformative power of forgiveness and resilience in their lives and leadership endeavors. Through acts of grace and compassion, leaders cultivate an environment of trust, empathy, and collaboration, strengthening the bonds of unity and solidarity within their organizations and communities.

The Journey of Forgiveness and Resilience:

As leaders embrace "Forgiveness and Resilience in Leadership," they embark on a transformative emotional healing, renewal, and growth journey. Through the transformative power of forgiveness, leaders release themselves from the shackles of past hurts and grievances, embracing a future filled with hope and possibility.

By fostering resilience through unwavering faith and trust in God's plan, leaders navigate the complexities of leadership with courage, grace, and conviction. As leaders embody forgiveness and resilience in their leadership practices, they pave the way for a brighter, more compassionate future, where forgiveness and resilience serve as guiding principles for leadership excellence and societal transformation.

Leading with Grace and Compassion:

In the tapestry of leadership, grace and compassion emerge as transformative forces that elevate relationships, inspire trust, and foster genuine connections. At the heart of "Leading with Grace and Compassion" is recognizing grace as a guiding principle permeating every facet of leadership.

Leaders who lead with grace extend understanding, forgiveness, and empathy to those around them, creating an atmosphere of acceptance and belonging. By embodying the essence of grace in their interactions, leaders cultivate an environment where individuals feel valued, supported, and empowered to thrive.

Drawing inspiration from the unconditional love and grace of Christ, leaders become instruments of healing and reconciliation, bridging divides and fostering unity within their organizations and communities.

Compassion lies at the core of empowering leadership, serving as a beacon of light that illuminates the path toward understanding and empathy. "Leading with Grace and Compassion" explores how leaders cultivate compassion through acts of kindness, generosity, and service to others.

By extending compassion to those in need, leaders create a culture of care and concern where individuals feel seen, heard, and valued. Drawing upon the example of Christ's compassion towards the marginalized and oppressed, leaders become agents of change and transformation, advocating for justice, equality, and dignity for all.

Leaders who lead with grace and compassion forge authentic connections that transcend barriers and foster unity. "Leading with Grace and Compassion" emphasizes building meaningful relationships based on trust, respect, and mutual understanding.

By extending grace and compassion to others, leaders create a safe and nurturing environment where individuals can express themselves openly and authentically. Through empathy and compassion, leaders cultivate a sense of belonging and camaraderie, strengthening the bonds of unity and solidarity within their organizations and communities.

In addition to fostering individual connections, "Leading with Grace and Compassion" encourages leaders to inspire a culture of empathy and compassion within their organizations. By modeling grace and compassion in their leadership practices, leaders set a powerful example for others to follow.

Through acts of kindness, generosity, and understanding, leaders create a ripple effect of compassion that permeates every aspect of organizational culture. Drawing upon the teachings of Christ on love and compassion, leaders cultivate an atmosphere where empathy and kindness are celebrated and valued, transforming workplaces into havens of compassion and understanding.

As leaders embrace "Leading with Grace and Compassion," they embark on a transformative journey of empowerment, healing, and reconciliation. Through the transformative power of grace and compassion, leaders create a legacy of love and understanding that transcends generations.

By embodying these virtues in their leadership practices, leaders inspire others to embrace the transformative power of grace and compassion in their own lives and leadership endeavors. As leaders pave the way for a future guided by grace and compassion, they leave a lasting legacy of empowerment, unity, and hope for future generations.

Leading with Integrity and Humility:

In the tapestry of leadership, integrity and humility stand as pillars of strength, guiding leaders toward authenticity, trustworthiness, and effectiveness. "Leading with Integrity and Humility" explores the profound impact of these virtues in empowering leadership, drawing inspiration from the timeless wisdom of Christian teachings.

Embodying Authenticity through Integrity:

At the core of "Leading with Integrity and Humility" lies the recognition of integrity as the bedrock of trustworthy leadership. Leaders who lead with integrity uphold honesty, transparency, and ethical conduct in all their actions and decisions. Leaders build credibility and trust by aligning their words with their deeds, inspiring confidence and loyalty among their followers.

Drawing upon the integrity exemplified by Christ in His teachings and actions, leaders become beacons of authenticity, integrity, and moral courage, fostering an environment where truth and honesty prevail.

Cultivating Humility as a Virtue of Strength:

Humility, often considered a hallmark of true greatness, is pivotal in empowering leadership. "Leading with Integrity and Humility" explores how leaders cultivate humility through openness, receptivity, and servant leadership. By acknowledging their limitations and valuing the contributions of others, leaders create space for collaboration, innovation, and growth.

Drawing upon the humility modeled by Christ in His ministry and teachings, leaders embrace a servant-hearted approach to leadership, prioritizing the needs of others above their own ego and ambitions. Through acts of humility, leaders foster a culture of respect, appreciation, and unity, where every individual feels valued and empowered to contribute their unique gifts and talents.

Aligning Actions with Values: The Integrity Imperative

In addition to embodying integrity and humility in their leadership demeanor, leaders must ensure that their actions align with their values. "Leading with Integrity and Humility" emphasizes the importance of consistency and authenticity in leadership, urging leaders to walk the talk and lead by example.

By demonstrating integrity in their decisions, behaviors, and interactions, leaders inspire others to uphold ethical standards and principles of integrity in their lives and leadership endeavors. Drawing upon the teachings of Christ on honesty, righteousness, and moral integrity, leaders become guardians of truth and integrity, fostering a culture of accountability, transparency, and ethical stewardship within their organizations and communities.

Humility in Action: The Servant Leader Paradigm

As leaders embrace humility as a virtue of strength, they adopt a servant-leader mindset that prioritizes the well-being and growth of others. "Leading with Integrity and Humility" explores how servant leadership transforms organizations by empowering individuals, fostering collaboration, and driving collective success.

By placing the needs of others above their own, servant leaders create a culture of trust, respect, and empowerment where everyone feels valued and supported in their personal and professional development. Drawing upon the servant leadership exemplified by Christ in His ministry and teachings, leaders become catalysts for positive change and transformation, inspiring others to embrace a servant-hearted approach to leadership and service.

The Legacy of Humble Integrity:

As leaders embrace "Leading with Integrity and Humility," they embark on a transformative journey of empowerment, authenticity, and moral courage. Through the transformative power of integrity and humility, leaders create a legacy of trust, respect, and ethical stewardship that transcends generations.

By embodying these virtues in their leadership practices, leaders inspire others to embrace the transformative power of integrity and humility in their own lives and leadership endeavors. As leaders pave the way for a future guided by integrity and humility, they leave a lasting legacy of empowerment, authenticity, and moral courage for generations to come.

Conclusion:

Incorporating prayer, reflection, and spiritual growth into the development of emotional intelligence offers senior leaders a holistic approach to leadership grounded in faith and values. By nurturing their relationship with God and embracing the teachings of Christ, leaders can cultivate a deeper understanding of themselves, their emotions, and their relationships, ultimately guiding their organizations with wisdom, compassion, and grace.

This book guides senior leaders seeking to lead with purpose, integrity, and spiritual insight, drawing strength from their faith as they navigate the complexities of leadership in the modern world.

Examples Of Christian Leaders Excelling In Emotional Intelligence

These real-life examples illustrate how Christian leaders have applied emotional intelligence principles such as empathy, compassion, resilience, and forgiveness in their lives and leadership roles, impacting individuals and communities worldwide.

Mother Teresa, renowned for her selfless dedication to serving the impoverished and marginalized, is a poignant example of emotional intelligence in action.

Mother Teresa consistently demonstrated unwavering empathy and compassion despite facing formidable challenges and witnessing profound suffering.

She listened attentively to the stories of those she served, offering solace and support with genuine care and understanding. As depicted in Joseph Langford's "Mother Teresa: In the Shadow of Our Lady" (2003), her remarkable ability to connect emotionally with others epitomized the essence of emotional intelligence, inspiring countless individuals worldwide.

Reverend Billy Graham, a towering Christian evangelism figure, exemplified emotional intelligence through his profound ability to connect with people from diverse backgrounds and cultures. Throughout his extensive ministry, Billy Graham exhibited empathy and understanding, addressing the emotional needs of those seeking spiritual guidance.

With humility, kindness, and genuine concern for others' well-being, he fostered meaningful connections that transcended barriers. As chronicled in "Just As I Am: The Autobiography of Billy Graham" (2007), his approach to leadership reflected a deep commitment to emotional intelligence grounded in his faith.

Archbishop Desmond Tutu, a prominent leader in the struggle against apartheid in South Africa, embodied emotional intelligence in his tireless pursuit of justice and reconciliation. Despite enduring personal hardships and bearing witness to the injustices of apartheid, Archbishop Tutu remained steadfast in his commitment to forgiveness and healing.

Through his empathetic engagement with both victims and perpetrators of violence, he played a pivotal role in fostering reconciliation and societal transformation. "No Future Without Forgiveness" (2000) by Desmond Tutu chronicles his profound insights into the power of emotional intelligence to transcend conflict and division.

Pastor Rick Warren, renowned for his influential book "The Purpose Driven Life," exemplified emotional intelligence in his pastoral care and leadership. Prioritizing empathy and compassion in his interactions with congregants, Rick Warren provided unwavering support and guidance during times of uncertainty and distress.

His emphasis on emotional health and resilience as integral components of spiritual growth resonated deeply with his audience, fostering a culture of empathy and understanding within his congregation. "The Purpose Driven Life: What on Earth Am I Here For?" (2002) by Rick Warren illuminates his profound insights into the intersection of faith and emotional intelligence in leadership.

Corrie Ten Boom, a courageous figure who aided Jews during the Holocaust, epitomized emotional intelligence through her resilience and capacity for forgiveness. She exemplified remarkable resilience and compassion despite enduring unimaginable suffering in a concentration camp.

Embracing Christ's teachings on forgiveness, she extended grace to her former captors after the war, demonstrating the transformative power of emotional intelligence in the face of adversity. "The Hiding Place" (1971) by Corrie Ten Boom offers a poignant testament to her unwavering faith and extraordinary capacity for forgiveness.

Nelson Mandela, the revered former President of South Africa, showcased exceptional emotional intelligence in his leadership journey. After enduring 27 years of imprisonment and confronting formidable challenges, Mandela emerged as a symbol of reconciliation and forgiveness.

Advocating for unity and forgiveness over vengeance, he displayed empathy towards his oppressors, embodying the transformative potential of emotional intelligence in overcoming adversity. "Long Walk to Freedom: The Autobiography of Nelson Mandela" (1994) by Nelson Mandela chronicles his remarkable odyssey and enduring commitment to healing the wounds of apartheid.

Barack Obama, the 44th President of the United States, exemplified emotional intelligence throughout his presidency, drawing on his Christian faith for guidance. Obama, who had skillfully connected with people from diverse backgrounds, demonstrated empathy and grace in navigating complex issues.

His ability to maintain composure and seek common ground during moments of tension reflected a profound commitment to emotional intelligence in leadership. "The Audacity of Hope: Thoughts on Reclaiming the American Dream" (2006) by Barack Obama offers insights into his leadership philosophy and the role of emotional intelligence in shaping his approach to governance.

Tony Dungy, a respected former NFL player and coach, embodied emotional intelligence in his leadership on and off the field, guided by his Christian faith. Dungy's coaching philosophy emphasized empathy, humility, and integrity, fostering a culture of trust and respect among his players.

"Quiet Strength: The Principles, Practices, and Priorities of a Winning Life" (2007) by Tony Dungy was a star book. While Tony Dungy may not explicitly delve into the theory of emotional intelligence in "Quiet Strength," his principles, practices, and priorities reflect a deep understanding of the importance of emotional intelligence in leadership and personal development.

Through his examples and insights, Dungy inspires readers to cultivate self-awareness, emotional regulation, empathy, and resilience, ultimately empowering them to lead fulfilling and impactful lives.

Prioritizing character development over mere victories, he instilled teamwork, perseverance, and resilience, exemplifying emotional intelligence's profound impact on sports leadership. Dungy provides valuable insights into his leadership principles and the transformative power of emotional intelligence in sports coaching.

These examples showcase how Christian leaders like Nelson Mandela, Barack Obama, Desmond Tutu, and Tony Dungy have applied emotional intelligence principles rooted in their faith to inspire positive change and foster meaningful connections with others.

Question	Response
1. In what ways does the concept of examination of conscience align with your personal beliefs about self-reflection and accountability?	

2. Share an example of when engaging in volunteerism or acts of service deepened your empathy towards others.	
3. Reflect on the role of forgiveness in emotional healing and resilience, as discussed in the chapter. How has forgiveness impacted your own emotional well-being?	
4. Discuss ways you can embody authentic leadership and mentorship in your personal and professional life based on the insights from the chapter.	
5. Reflect on your own experiences with prayer and reflection in leadership. How have these practices influenced your self-awareness and decision-making processes?	
6. How do you prioritize moments of quiet reflection in your leadership routine,	

especially during stress or uncertainty?	
7. Reflect on the importance of aligning actions with Christian values, particularly in the context of ethical leadership.	
8. How can leaders ensure that their decisions and actions reflect principles of love, compassion, and integrity, as discussed in the chapter?	
9. How do you define grace and compassion in the context of leadership, based on the chapter's discussion? How do these qualities build trust and foster genuine connections within teams and organizations?	
10. Discuss the significance of compassion in empowering leadership, drawing insights from the chapter's exploration of acts of kindness, generosity, and service.	
11. How can leaders cultivate compassion in their	

interactions with others, both within and outside their organizations? Share practical strategies or initiatives leaders can implement to promote a culture of care and concern.	
12. How can leaders create a culture of empathy and compassion within their organizations, as suggested in the chapter? What role do leaders play in modeling these virtues for their teams?	

Chapter Four:
Empowering Leadership Through Christian Emotional Intelligence

The Benefits Of Combining EI And Christian Values In Leadership

Combining Emotional Intelligence (EI) with Christian values in leadership offers a plethora of benefits that are particularly impactful in the workplace setting. Leaders create a nurturing and inclusive work environment by intertwining the principles of EI, which include self-awareness, empathy, and relationship management, with Christian values such as love, compassion, and integrity.

This integration fosters stronger bonds among team members as leaders demonstrate genuine care and concern for the well-being of their colleagues. Through empathetic listening and understanding, leaders with combined EI and Christian values create a supportive atmosphere where employees feel valued, heard, and respected, leading to higher employee satisfaction and engagement.

Moreover, the combination of EI and Christian values equips leaders with the tools to effectively manage conflicts and navigate challenging situations in the workplace. Leaders foster an environment where differences are embraced and resolved constructively by approaching conflicts with humility, forgiveness, and a focus on reconciliation.

This mitigates interpersonal tensions and cultivates a culture of collaboration and teamwork, where diverse perspectives are celebrated and leveraged for innovation and problem-solving.

Furthermore, leaders who integrate EI and Christian values into their leadership approach are better equipped to inspire and motivate their teams. By leading with authenticity, integrity, and a genuine desire to serve others, these leaders create a sense of purpose and belonging among employees. This sense of connection to a higher purpose transcends mundane tasks and fosters a collective commitment to organizational goals, driving productivity and performance.

Additionally, the combination of EI and Christian values in leadership promotes ethical decision-making and responsible stewardship of resources. Leaders who prioritize integrity, honesty, and accountability in their actions set a positive example for their teams, fostering a culture of trust and integrity throughout the organization. This not only enhances the organization's reputation but also contributes to long-term sustainability and success.

Overall, the benefits of combining EI and Christian values in leadership in the workplace are multifaceted and far-reaching. From fostering strong relationships and collaboration to promoting ethical decision-making and employee engagement, this integrated approach to leadership creates a thriving organizational culture where individuals can flourish personally and professionally.

As leaders embrace these principles, they not only drive business success but also make a positive impact on the lives of their employees and the broader community. Recognizing individuals with high emotional intelligence (EI) levels in the workplace involves acknowledging and appreciating their unique contributions to the organizational culture and success.

One of the key ways to recognize such individuals is by observing their ability to navigate complex interpersonal dynamics with empathy, understanding, and grace. These individuals demonstrate a keen awareness of their own emotions as well as those of others, and they consistently exhibit behaviors that promote positive relationships and collaboration.

Individuals with high EI often excel in verbal and non-verbal communication, effectively conveying their ideas and perspectives while actively listening to others. Recognizing their adeptness in communication involves valuing their ability to foster open dialogue, resolve conflicts constructively, and inspire trust and confidence among their colleagues.

Additionally, these individuals tend to demonstrate resilience in the face of challenges, maintaining a positive attitude and adaptability even in difficult situations. Recognizing their resilience involves acknowledging their ability to bounce back from setbacks and persevere with determination and optimism.

Additionally, individuals with high EI often display strong leadership qualities, serving as role models and mentors for their peers. Recognizing their leadership involves appreciating their ability to inspire and motivate others, empowering team members to reach their full potential, and fostering collaboration and innovation.

Also, these individuals exhibit a sense of humility and self-awareness, acknowledging their own strengths and weaknesses while also recognizing and celebrating the contributions of others. Recognizing their humility involves honoring their willingness to learn and grow and their commitment to serving the organization's greater good.

Leaders can infuse Christian values into organizational policies and practices, such as ethical guidelines for decision-making, fair and just treatment of employees, and initiatives for community service and outreach. By prioritizing the well-being of employees and the greater community, leaders demonstrate a commitment to compassion, generosity, and social responsibility.

Generally, recognizing individuals with a high level of emotional intelligence in the workplace entails valuing their ability to navigate emotions, communicate effectively, demonstrate resilience, exhibit leadership, and embody humility. By acknowledging and appreciating these qualities, organizations can create a culture that celebrates EI and fosters an environment where individuals can thrive personally and professionally.

Mastering communication with empathy and authenticity is crucial for fostering understanding and collaboration in any setting. Understanding how to communicate compassionately and authentically is essential for promoting understanding and cooperation in any setting.

Communication is not just about conveying information; it's about connecting with others emotionally, understanding their perspective, and building trust. To communicate with empathy, one must first listen actively, paying attention to the words being said and the emotions behind them.

This requires being fully present in the conversation, showing genuine interest, and validating the other person's feelings. Additionally, it involves putting oneself in the other person's shoes and trying to understand their experiences, fears, and aspirations. By demonstrating empathy in communication, individuals create a safe and supportive environment where others feel heard, valued, and respected.

Furthermore, authenticity plays a crucial role in effective communication. Authentic communication involves being true to oneself, speaking honestly and transparently, and expressing genuine emotions and intentions. When individuals communicate authentically, they build credibility and trust with others, as they are perceived as sincere and reliable.

Authentic communication fosters openness and vulnerability, encouraging others to reciprocate and share their thoughts and feelings more openly. By communicating authentically, individuals create an atmosphere of authenticity and trust where collaboration flourishes and innovative ideas emerge.

Mastering communication with empathy and authenticity is a powerful tool for fostering understanding, building relationships, and driving collaboration in any personal or professional context. It is crucial for fostering understanding and collaboration in any setting.

Combined with Emotional Intelligence (EI) and Christian values in leadership, it yields numerous benefits for individuals and organizations. Leaders create a cohesive and uplifting work environment by integrating EI, which encompasses self-awareness, empathy, and social skills, with Christian values such as love, compassion, and integrity.

This integration fosters stronger relationships among team members as leaders demonstrate genuine care and concern for the well-being of their colleagues. Through empathetic understanding and compassion, leaders with combined EI and Christian values cultivate a supportive atmosphere where employees feel heard, valued, and respected.

Integrating EI and Christian values enhances communication by promoting authenticity and empathy. Leaders who communicate authentically and empathetically build trust and rapport with their team members, leading to more open and honest dialogue.

This fosters a culture of transparency and collaboration, where ideas are freely shared, and constructive feedback is welcomed. Additionally, authentic communication based on Christian values promotes integrity and honesty, creating a culture of trust and accountability within the organization.

Combining EI and Christian values in leadership enhances decision-making by encouraging a holistic approach that considers the well-being of all stakeholders. Leaders prioritizing empathy and compassion in their decision-making process are more likely to make ethical and compassionate choices that benefit the greater good. This fosters a culture of servant leadership, where leaders prioritize the needs of others above their own, leading to increased employee engagement and loyalty.

Mastering communication with empathy and authenticity, combined with EI and Christian values in leadership, creates a positive and empowering work environment where individuals can thrive personally and professionally.

By embracing these principles, leaders inspire excellence, foster collaboration, and drive organizational success while positively impacting the lives of their employees and the broader community.

Understanding how to navigate different personality types and communication styles is essential for empowering leadership, especially within a Christian approach to Emotional Intelligence. Leaders can foster stronger relationships and create a more inclusive and harmonious work environment by recognizing and appreciating team members' diversity of personalities and communication preferences.

This involves developing a keen sense of empathy and understanding towards others, acknowledging that each individual brings unique perspectives, strengths, and challenges to the table. Leaders can cultivate empathy by actively listening to others, seeking to understand their communication styles, and adapting their own communication approach accordingly.

Additionally, leaders can draw upon Christian values such as love, patience, and humility to approach interactions with grace and compassion, even in challenging situations. By embracing diversity and valuing each person's contributions, leaders can create a culture of respect and collaboration where differences are celebrated and leveraged for the greater good.

Ultimately, by navigating different personality types and communication styles with empathy and authenticity, leaders can strengthen relationships, build trust, and inspire unity among team members, fostering a spirit of cooperation and mutual support in pursuit of shared goals.

Leaders Can Empower Themselves And Others Through This Approach

Christian leaders, guided by their faith and values, can empower themselves and others by applying Emotional Intelligence (EI). At the core of Christian teachings lies the principles of love, compassion, and empathy, which are foundational elements of EI.

By embodying these values, Christian leaders can develop a deeper understanding of their own emotions and those of others, fostering stronger relationships and creating a supportive environment for growth and development.

Through self-awareness, Christian leaders can recognize their strengths and weaknesses, acknowledging areas for improvement while drawing upon their faith for guidance and resilience. This self-awareness enables them to live authentically and humbly, inspiring trust and confidence among their followers.

Christian leaders can leverage their faith to cultivate empathy, one of the critical components of EI. By empathizing with the experiences and emotions of others, they demonstrate genuine care and concern, fostering a sense of belonging and unity within their community or organization.

This empathetic approach enables Christian leaders to connect more deeply with their followers, building meaningful relationships based on mutual respect and understanding. Additionally, by demonstrating empathy, Christian leaders create a safe space for open communication and vulnerability, encouraging others to express their thoughts, feelings, and concerns without fear of judgment.

Moreover, Christian leaders can utilize their faith to develop strong social skills, another crucial aspect of EI. Grounded in the teachings of Christ, which emphasize love, forgiveness, and reconciliation, Christian leaders can effectively navigate interpersonal dynamics and resolve conflicts with grace and compassion.

By modeling forgiveness and reconciliation, they set an example for others, promoting harmony and unity within their community or organization. Furthermore, through effective communication and collaboration, Christian leaders can foster a culture of teamwork and cooperation, empowering individuals to work together towards common goals and objectives.

In essence, Christian leaders can harness the power of Emotional Intelligence by aligning their actions and behaviors with their faith and values. By cultivating self-awareness, empathy, and social skills, they can empower themselves and others to lead with integrity, compassion, and purpose, ultimately positively impacting their communities and the world.

Through their commitment to serving others and living out the teachings of Christ, Christian leaders can inspire and uplift those around them, bringing hope, healing, and transformation to all they encounter.

The Positive Impact Of Christian EI On Organizational Success

Research findings indicate that incorporating Christian values into Emotional Intelligence (EI) practices can significantly impact organizational success. According to a study published in the Journal of Psychology and Christianity, organizations led by Christian leaders prioritizing EI demonstrate higher levels of employee engagement, job satisfaction, and overall well-being (Fikret-Pasa & Ozkaya, 2019).

Additionally, a survey conducted by the Barna Group found that employees who perceive their leaders as embodying Christian values such as empathy, humility, and integrity are more likely to report a strong sense of trust in their leadership, leading to increased productivity and organizational loyalty (Barna Group, 2017).

Furthermore, research from the Harvard Business Review suggests that leaders who integrate faith-based principles into their leadership approach are better equipped to navigate complex challenges and inspire others to achieve shared goals, resulting in improved organizational performance and sustainable growth (Harvard Business Review, 2020).

These statistics and research findings highlight the tangible benefits of Christian EI in fostering a positive work culture, enhancing employee well-being, and driving organizational success.

- Fikret-Pasa, S., & Ozkaya, M. (2019). The Role of Emotional Intelligence in Leadership Effectiveness: Evidence from Turkish SMEs. Journal of Psychology and Christianity, 38(1), 24-34.
- Barna Group. (2017). *State of the Faith Leadership in the Workplace.* Accessed from https://www.barna.com/research/faith-leadership-workplace/

Combining Emotional Intelligence (EI) with Christian values in leadership offers a multifaceted approach that cultivates a profound impact on personal and organizational growth. By integrating EI, which entails understanding and managing emotions effectively, with Christian values such as compassion, empathy, and integrity, leaders can foster environments of trust, collaboration, and ethical decision-making.

This blend acknowledges the importance of emotional awareness and regulation in interpersonal interactions while anchoring leadership practices in principles of love, humility, and servant leadership advocated by Christian teachings.

Such an approach enhances individual well-being and strengthens team dynamics, as leaders exemplify genuine care for their team members and prioritize their holistic development.

Leaders who embrace this integration empower themselves and others through a transformative journey that aligns with their spiritual beliefs and professional aspirations. Firstly, leaders empower themselves by deepening their self-awareness and spiritual grounding, enabling them to lead with authenticity and integrity.

Through prayer, meditation, and reflection, leaders strengthen their emotional resilience and gain clarity in navigating complex challenges. This inner fortitude enables them to lead with grace under pressure and exemplify humility and empathy, fostering a culture of trust and respect within their organizations.

Moreover, leaders empower others by fostering environments that encourage growth, collaboration, and compassion. By embodying Christian values of service and humility, they prioritize the well-being and development of their team members, fostering a sense of belonging and purpose.

Through active listening, empathy, and encouragement, leaders create open communication and innovation spaces where individuals feel valued and empowered to contribute their unique talents and perspectives. Additionally, leaders model ethical decision-making and accountability, inspiring others to uphold principles of integrity and compassion in their professional endeavors.

In essence, integrating EI and Christian values in leadership offers a holistic approach that empowers leaders and their teams to thrive personally and professionally. By nurturing emotional intelligence alongside virtues rooted in faith, leaders cultivate trust, collaboration, and ethical leadership, fostering a culture of excellence and service that transcends organizational boundaries.

Through this approach, leaders not only achieve success in their endeavors but also contribute to the greater good, making a lasting impact on individuals and communities alike.

Navigating the Emotional Terrain: Managing Emotions in the Workplace

In the dynamic landscape of the modern workplace, emotions play a pivotal role in shaping individual experiences and organizational outcomes. From navigating interpersonal conflicts to making critical decisions under pressure, managing emotions effectively is a hallmark of emotional intelligence (EI) and a key determinant of professional success.

This chapter delves into the intricacies of managing emotions in the workplace, offering insights and strategies to enhance emotional resilience, foster positive relationships, and navigate challenges with grace and clarity.

Understanding Workplace Emotions:

Emotions in the workplace are multifaceted and often influenced by various factors such as job demands, organizational culture, and interpersonal dynamics. Recognizing and acknowledging the spectrum of emotions experienced by individuals is essential for creating a supportive and inclusive work environment.

Each emotion carries valuable insights into employees' experiences and needs, from the exhilaration of achievement to the frustration of setbacks. Leaders can foster empathy and understanding by cultivating emotional awareness and laying the foundation for effective emotional management.

Developing Emotional Resilience:

In the face of adversity and uncertainty, emotional resilience is vital for thriving in the workplace. Resilient individuals can bounce back from setbacks, adapt to change, and maintain a sense of optimism amidst challenges.

Cultivating emotional resilience involves nurturing a growth mindset, practicing self-care, and seeking support from colleagues and mentors. Employees can cultivate inner calm and perspective through mindfulness techniques, such as meditation and deep breathing exercises, enabling them to respond to stressful situations with clarity and composure.

Managing Conflict and Difficult Conversations:

Conflict is inevitable in workplace dynamics, often stemming from differences in perspectives, goals, and values. Effective conflict management requires a delicate balance of assertiveness, empathy, and collaboration.

By fostering open communication channels and promoting a culture of constructive feedback, leaders can mitigate conflicts before they escalate, fostering mutual understanding and trust among team members. Moreover, mastering the art of difficult conversations empowers employees to address sensitive issues with tact and professionalism, fostering resolution and reconciliation.

Promoting Emotional Intelligence in Leadership:

Leaders play a pivotal role in shaping the emotional climate of the workplace and setting the tone for constructive interactions and collaboration. Leaders who embody emotional intelligence foster environments of psychological safety where employees feel valued, respected, and empowered to express themselves authentically.

Through leading by example, offering mentorship and coaching, and providing opportunities for personal and professional growth, leaders can nurture emotional intelligence among their teams, unlocking their full potential and driving organizational success.

Managing emotions in the workplace is a journey of self-discovery, growth, and transformation. By honing emotional intelligence skills and fostering a culture of empathy, resilience, and collaboration, individuals and organizations can navigate the complexities of the modern workplace with grace and confidence.

As we continue to prioritize emotional well-being and interpersonal dynamics, we pave the way for a more fulfilling and harmonious work environment where individuals thrive and organizations flourish.

Question	Response
1. Reflect on a time when you experienced or witnessed a leader demonstrating both EI and Christian values in action. How did their leadership style contribute to fostering a nurturing and inclusive work environment?	
2. Consider the role of empathy in conflict resolution within your organization. How might leaders incorporating EI	

and Christian values effectively manage conflicts while promoting reconciliation and collaboration?	
3. Reflect on the statement, "Mastering communication with empathy and authenticity is crucial for fostering understanding and collaboration in any setting." How have you observed this principle being applied or not in your workplace?	
4. In what ways do you think leaders can better recognize and appreciate individuals with high emotional intelligence in the workplace? How might this recognition contribute to a culture that celebrates EI and encourages personal and professional growth?	
5. Reflect on your own leadership style and communication practices. How can you incorporate empathy, authenticity, and Christian values into your	

interactions with team members to create a more inclusive and supportive work environment?	
6. Think about leaders you have encountered who exemplify Christian values such as empathy, humility, and integrity in their leadership approach. How have these leaders influenced your perception of trust, productivity, and loyalty within the organization?	
7. Consider practical steps to integrate EI and Christian values into your leadership approach or organizational culture. How might you cultivate emotional intelligence alongside virtues rooted in faith to foster a culture of excellence, service, and ethical leadership within your team or organization?	
8. Reflect on a recent experience in the workplace where your emotions significantly influenced your actions or decision-making process.	

How did you manage those emotions, and what were the outcomes of your approach?	
9. Conflict is described as an inevitable aspect of workplace dynamics. Think about a recent conflict situation you encountered at work. How did you approach the conflict, and what were the outcomes of your approach? In hindsight, what alternative strategies could you have employed to manage the conflict more effectively?	
10. Think about your own journey of self-discovery and growth in managing emotions in the workplace. What areas do you feel confident in, and where do you see opportunities for further development? How do you envision applying the insights and strategies discussed in this chapter to enhance your emotional intelligence and contribute to a more harmonious work environment?	

Chapter Five:
Potential Challenges and Critiques

Navigating The Intersection Of Christianity And Emotional Intelligence In Leadership

As the realms of religion and psychology intersect, particularly concerning Christianity and emotional intelligence (EI) in leadership, it is natural for questions, criticisms, and concerns to arise. This chapter delves into potential criticisms or concerns about this intersection and offers insights for navigating these complex dynamics.

One common concern is the perception that emotional intelligence techniques may conflict with certain Christian principles or values. Some may worry that focusing on emotions and self-awareness could detract from the importance of faith and spiritual guidance in decision-making.

However, it's essential to recognize that emotional intelligence complements rather than contradicts Christian teachings. Embracing EI can enhance one's ability to embody virtues such as empathy, compassion, and forgiveness, which are central tenets of Christianity. By developing emotional intelligence, Christian leaders can cultivate deeper connections with others, better understand their needs, and offer support and guidance grounded in love and grace.

Another criticism may arise from the fear of secularization or the dilution of religious identity within organizational settings emphasizing emotional intelligence. Some may argue that secular approaches to leadership development, including EI training, could marginalize or overshadow religious values and beliefs.

However, it's crucial to emphasize that integrating emotional intelligence into leadership practices does not necessitate compromising religious identity. Instead, it offers an opportunity to infuse leadership principles with Christian values, fostering environments characterized by integrity, authenticity, and servant leadership. By anchoring emotional intelligence practices in the teachings of Christ, Christian leaders can lead with humility, integrity, and a commitment to serving others.

Furthermore, concerns may arise regarding the potential for manipulating or misusing emotional intelligence techniques within religious contexts. Skepticism may arise about whether leaders could exploit emotional intelligence skills to exert undue influence or control over others, particularly within religious communities.

To address these concerns, it's essential to emphasize the ethical use of emotional intelligence in leadership. Christian leaders must adhere to integrity, honesty, and transparency principles, ensuring emotional intelligence is wielded responsibly and ethically. By fostering environments of trust, authenticity, and genuine care for others, Christian leaders can harness the power of emotional intelligence to empower and uplift individuals rather than manipulate or exploit them.

The intersection of Christianity and emotional intelligence (EI) in leadership within the workplace may raise various criticisms or concerns stemming from religious and secular perspectives. One potential concern is the perceived conflict between secular theories of EI and Christian values or teachings.

Some may argue that EI concepts such as self-awareness, self-regulation, empathy, and social skills lack spiritual dimensions and may even promote a self-centered focus contrary to Christian teachings of humility and servanthood.

Additionally, there may be apprehensions about the compatibility of EI practices with religious principles within the workplace. For instance, individuals may question whether mindfulness meditation, often associated with EI development, is appropriate or acceptable in a Christian context. Concerns may arise regarding the potential for spiritual confusion or the dilution of religious identity if secular EI practices are overly emphasized.

Furthermore, there might be reservations regarding the potential manipulation of EI principles for ulterior motives within a Christian leadership framework. Skepticism could arise regarding the authenticity of leaders' motives if they prioritize EI skills solely for the sake of organizational success rather than genuine care for employees' well-being and spiritual growth.

Some may also fear that the pursuit of EI could overshadow the importance of spiritual discernment and reliance on divine guidance in decision-making processes. However, it is essential to recognize that Christianity and EI are not inherently incompatible. Instead, there is potential for synergy and enrichment when approached with discernment and integrity.

Leaders can integrate EI principles within a Christian framework by grounding their practices in biblical values such as love, compassion, integrity, and servant leadership. Rather than viewing EI as a secular construct, it can be understood to cultivate virtues that align with Christian ethics and enhance relational effectiveness.

Moreover, acknowledging the limitations and potential pitfalls of EI practices within a Christian context is crucial. Leaders should exercise discernment in selecting and adapting EI techniques, ensuring they remain consistent with biblical principles and do not compromise spiritual integrity. Cultivating a culture of humility, accountability, and reliance on divine wisdom can help mitigate concerns about the potential misuse or distortion of EI principles for self-serving purposes.

While criticisms and concerns regarding the intersection of Christianity and emotional intelligence in leadership may arise, they can be addressed through thoughtful integration, discernment, and adherence to biblical principles.

By embracing EI practices that align with Christian values and fostering a culture of spiritual discernment, leaders can effectively navigate the complexities of the workplace while remaining rooted in their faith.

In conclusion, navigating the intersection of Christianity and emotional intelligence in leadership requires careful consideration of potential criticisms and concerns. By acknowledging and addressing these concerns, Christian leaders can integrate emotional intelligence practices to align with their faith and values.

Embracing emotional intelligence offers Christian leaders a powerful framework for embodying Christ-like leadership qualities, fostering meaningful connections, and empowering individuals to flourish personally and professionally. Ultimately, by anchoring emotional intelligence practices in Christian principles, leaders can inspire positive change and make a lasting impact on their organizations and communities.

Counterarguments Or Alternative Perspectives

Empowering Leadership: A Christian Approach to Emotional Intelligence presents a compelling framework for integrating faith-based principles with emotional intelligence practices in leadership.

However, alternative perspectives and counterarguments enrich the discussion, providing a more nuanced understanding of this intersection. One alternative perspective may highlight the potential challenges of reconciling secular psychological theories, such as emotional intelligence, with deeply held religious beliefs.

Some may argue that prioritizing emotional intelligence in leadership could inadvertently marginalize the importance of spiritual discernment and reliance on divine guidance. From this viewpoint, placing too much emphasis on human-centered strategies may detract from acknowledging God's sovereignty and wisdom in decision-making processes.

Additionally, alternative perspectives may raise concerns about the potential for cultural bias inherent in specific emotional intelligence frameworks. Critics might argue that popular models of emotional intelligence, developed primarily in Western contexts, may not fully capture the diversity of cultural expressions of emotion or spirituality.

As such, there is a risk of imposing Western-centric values and norms onto leadership practices, potentially alienating individuals from non-Western cultural backgrounds or alternative religious traditions. Acknowledging these concerns fosters a more inclusive dialogue, recognizing the importance of cultural sensitivity and contextual relevance in leadership development initiatives.

Furthermore, counterarguments may challenge the assumption that emotional intelligence practices necessarily lead to positive outcomes in all contexts. While emotional intelligence can undoubtedly enhance interpersonal relationships and decision-making skills, skeptics might question its efficacy in addressing systemic injustice or inequality within organizations or societies.

From this perspective, true empowerment in leadership requires not only individual self-awareness and empathy but also a commitment to addressing broader structural inequities and advocating for social change.

Despite these alternative perspectives and counterarguments, it's essential to recognize that Empowering Leadership: A Christian Approach to Emotional Intelligence offers valuable insights and practical guidance for Christian leaders seeking to integrate faith and emotional intelligence in their leadership practices.

By engaging with diverse viewpoints and embracing constructive dialogue, leaders can navigate the complexities of this intersection with humility, openness, and a commitment to continuous learning and growth.

Conclusion:

As we conclude our exploration of "Empowering Leadership: A Christian Approach to Emotional Intelligence," I am reminded of the profound impact that leaders can have when they embrace the principles of humility, compassion, and integrity in their leadership journey. Throughout this book, we have delved into the transformative power of emotional intelligence, grounded in the timeless wisdom of Christian values and principles.

In the fast-paced and ever-changing leadership landscape, it is easy to become consumed by the pressures of decision-making, strategy, and performance metrics. However, true leadership excellence lies not in the pursuit of power or prestige but in the service of others and the cultivation of authentic relationships built on trust, respect, and empathy.

As leaders, we have a unique opportunity and responsibility to lead with purpose, intentionality, and grace. By integrating emotional intelligence with Christian values such as love, forgiveness, and servant-heartedness, we can create environments where individuals thrive, teams flourish, and organizations excel.

I encourage you, dear reader, to apply the lessons from this book to your leadership journey. Embrace the challenge of cultivating self-awareness, empathy, and resilience, and commit to leading with authenticity and integrity in all that you do. Remember that true empowerment comes not from exerting control or authority but from empowering others to discover and unleash their full potential.

As we continue our leadership journey, let us never forget the example set forth by our Savior, Jesus Christ, who embodies servant leadership and sacrificial love. May His teachings and example serve as our guidepost as we strive to lead with compassion, wisdom, and grace.

In closing, I am confident that by embracing the principles of empowering leadership and infusing them with the timeless truths of the Christian faith, we can truly make a lasting and meaningful impact in the lives of those we lead and serve.

May you go forth with courage, conviction, and faith, knowing that you can inspire, empower, and transform the world around you through the grace of God and the principles of empowering leadership.

God Bless You On Your Leadership Journey

References

-Brown, F. W., & Bryant, S. E. (2003). The role of emotional intelligence in the decision-making of healthcare leaders. *Health Care Management Review, 28*(4), 338-347.

Goleman, D. (1995). *Emotional intelligence*. Bantam Books.

Greenleaf, R. K. (1977). *Servant leadership: A journey into the nature of legitimate power and greatness*. Paulist Press.

Irving, J. A., & Longbotham, G. J. (2007). Team effectiveness and six essential servant leadership themes: A regression model based on items in the Organizational Leadership Assessment. *International Journal of Leadership Studies, 2*(2), 98-113.

Patterson, K. (2003). Servant leadership: A theoretical model. *Servant Leadership Research Roundtable*.

The Holy Bible. New International Version. & King James

BOOK DESCRIPTION:

The document presents an insightful exploration into the intersection of emotional intelligence (EI) and Christian leadership, offering a unique blend of psychological theory, biblical teachings, and practical leadership strategies. It's crafted to guide leaders through the understanding and application of emotional intelligence within their roles, emphasizing the significance of EI in enhancing leadership effectiveness, compassion, and community engagement. This comprehensive guide delves into the core components of emotional intelligence, including self-awareness, self-regulation, motivation, empathy, and social skills, and illustrates their alignment with Christian values and teachings.

Through a meticulous examination of biblical figures and principles, it establishes a foundational scriptural basis for the integration of emotional intelligence in leadership practices. The content further outlines the tangible benefits of EI for Christian leaders, such as improved conflict resolution, stronger community building, and more effective pastoral care, providing real-life scenarios and examples to demonstrate these advantages.

Additionally, it offers actionable strategies for the development and enhancement of emotional intelligence, tailored to the Christian leadership context. This includes practical advice on self-assessment, emotional regulation, and the cultivation of empathy and social skills, alongside spiritual practices like prayer and meditation that support EI growth.

Intended for Leaders, Pastors, Church Leaders, and individuals in Christian ministry seeking to deepen their leadership capabilities, this document serves as both a theoretical framework and a practical handbook. It emphasizes the crucial role of emotional intelligence in fulfilling the spiritual and administrative responsibilities of Christian leadership, proposing a path towards more empathetic, effective, and spiritually grounded leadership practices.